Madeleine F. Wallace, PhD

THRIVE IN THE AI AND DIGITAL AGE:
The SEAM 4-Step
Career Guide & Workbook

THRIVE IN THE AI AND DIGITAL AGE:
The SEAM 4-Step
Career Guide & Workbook

For more information contact:

Email: mfw@madeleinewallace.com
https://www.madeleinewallace.com

All figures, tables, and career profile illustrations by Madeleine F. Wallace, Ph.D.

Cover Design and Layout by Fig Factor Media LLC
Printed in the United States of America

ISBN: 978-1-961600-43-0
Library of Congress Control Number: 2024916960

FIG FACTOR MEDIA

DEDICATION

To my rock, Stephen, my husband, whose boundless optimism lights up my darkest days, whose integrity fortifies my journey, and whose intelligence is both inspiring and infectious. His joy is uplifting, and his love is tangible in every action. His compassion and incredible imagination enrich our lives, and our shared love for adventure keeps our journey exciting. My parents always said that finding a partner with whom you can connect intellectually and professionally is a yapa—a little extra bonus in life, from the Quechua term, yapay. I am grateful for always supporting me in pursuing every professional dream, wanting me to shine brightly, and enabling me to support him in the same way.

TABLE OF CONTENTS

ACKNOWLEDGEMENTS

I am deeply grateful to my mentees, whose curiosity and drive to excel in diverse career paths inspired me to write this guide and workbook, dedicated to helping others fulfill their aspirations.

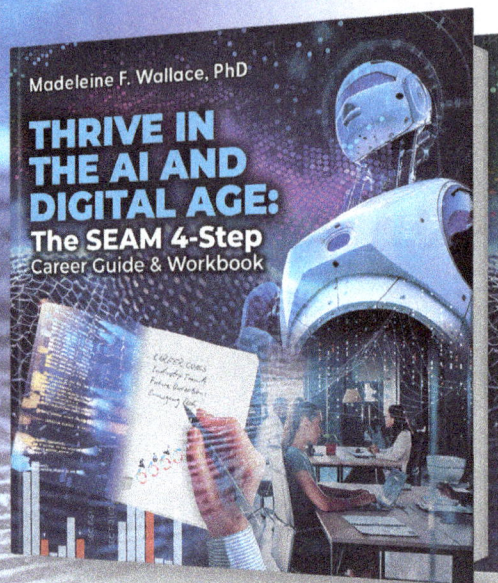

INTRODUCTION

With the rise of artificial intelligence (AI) and digital technologies, the job market is evolving faster than ever. It's time we evolved with it. Whether you're starting your career, considering a pivot due to shifting job demands, looking to boost your leadership skills, or even venturing into entrepreneurship, understanding and leveraging the latest technological trends are crucial.

INTRODUCING THRIVE IN THE AI AND DIGITAL AGE: THE SEAM 4-STEPS CAREER GUIDE AND WORKBOOK

What sets this comprehensive, interactive guide apart is its personalized approach. Through a series of self-assessments, you'll discover your unique career profile – one of seven carefully designed to reflect your current stage and aspirations. This profile will unlock a customized path of activities and exercises, ensuring the content is directly relevant to your unique needs and goals.

Packed with exercises, science-backed insights, personal anecdotes, and motivational content, this workbook teaches you to envision and achieve your future career with a dynamic, skills-based approach.

To accelerate your progress, we'll harness the power of Agile methodology, a proven approach used by top companies to drive innovation and adapt to change. You'll learn to break down your career goals into manageable "sprints," allowing you to experiment, learn, and iterate quickly.

You'll find additional resources both within this book and on my website, madeleinewallace.com. Throughout the process, you'll cultivate the adaptability, resilience, and forward-thinking mindset essential for thriving in an ever-changing professional landscape.

PREPARING FOR AN UNCERTAIN FUTURE: SCENARIO PLANNING

Being prepared for change is the key to thriving in today's dynamic world. That's why this workbook also introduces you to the power of scenario planning. By exploring best-case, worst-case, and balanced career scenarios, you'll build unshakeable resilience and the agility to pivot with confidence as circumstances evolve.

A PERSONAL JOURNEY

Witnessing how quickly technology can disrupt businesses and careers left a lasting impact on me. As a teenager, I saw my parents' thriving vocational school, which offered courses like shorthand, bookkeeping, and typing, struggle to survive as technology advanced. The rise of computers rendered some of their courses obsolete, leading them to close the school.

My parents adapted by shifting from being business owners to working for others. This experience underscored the importance of understanding and navigating technological disruption. It sparked my passion for organizational transformation and inspired my work through Windrose Vision (www.windrosevision.com), where I consult with organizations on adapting to change and equipping their teams with the tools to reskill and upskill in an evolving job market.

Like my parents, I am committed to mentoring others through their career development journeys—whether they are recent graduates, entrepreneurs, or professionals in transition. My mission is to empower people to stay relevant by continually enhancing their skills.

Beyond business, my purpose extends to advancing a more equitable future in education at Conectado (www.conectado.com) and training career administrators at leading universities through my work with the Burroughs Wellcome Fund.

THE SEAM FRAMEWORK

Your guide on this journey is the SEAM Framework, a proven catalyst for digital transformations in organizations that I introduced in my book, The SEAM Framework: Achieving Organizational Transformational in 4 Steps. SEAM stands for:

- **Snapshot:** Evaluate your skills and career through the lens of relevant trends, future directions, and emerging technologies.

- **Envision:** Imagine a dynamic future where you adapt, evolve, and align your goals with a changing career landscape.

- **Act:** Take purposeful, agile steps to evolve your career goals, using sprints to ensure continuous learning.

- **Measure:** Regularly assess your progress to stay on track and celebrate accomplishments.

My research on successful career development programs, particularly the NIH-funded Broadening Experience in Scientific Training (BEST) study (Lenzi et al., 2020), has directly informed the content of this workbook. Additionally, my work evaluating other NIH initiatives, such as the Early Independence Awards, the Building Interdisciplinary Research Careers in Women's Health program, and the NSF's ADVANCE program, has further enriched my understanding of what drives career success.

These studies have highlighted critical elements that are woven throughout the SEAM Career framework. Key factors include broadening awareness of career opportunities, enhancing decision-making skills, and fostering adaptability in an ever-evolving professional landscape. These insights are designed to equip individuals with the tools needed to navigate and thrive in their careers.

NAVIGATING CAREER STAGES WITH TECHNOLOGICAL INSIGHTS

The SEAM framework aligns perfectly with the shift towards skills-based hiring (Deloitte, 2022) and the impact of digital and AI technologies on the workplace (Microsoft, 2024). It provides a structured approach, offering targeted exercises, focus areas, and resources tailored to your career stage:

- **Early Career:** Launch your career with confidence. SEAM helps you craft a personalized career plan, acquire in-demand skills, and develop strategies to stay ahead of the curve in a rapidly evolving technological landscape.

- **Mid-Career Pivot:** Navigate transitions with purpose. SEAM guides you in identifying and leveraging your transferable skills, setting flexible and fixed goals to maintain momentum, and positioning yourself strategically for new opportunities.

- **Leadership / Senior Roles:** Lead and inspire in the digital age. SEAM offers valuable perspectives on continuous learning, fostering the development of new generations, and leaving a legacy in your field.

No matter where you are in your career journey, SEAM equips you with the tools and insights to not only survive but to thrive in an ever-changing professional world.

HOW TO USE THIS WORKBOOK

This workbook is designed to be an interactive tool that supports your career transformation journey. Here are some suggestions on how to make the most out of it:

- **Treat It as Your Career Journal:** Use the workbook to jot down your thoughts, ideas, and reflections. Write in the margins, scratch out ideas, and use the space to work through your thoughts. Engage with the Insight Exercises by writing directly in the workbook, even if you're using an app for tracking progress.

- **Download Additional Templates:** For more space to explore your ideas, download additional templates from my website: madeleinewallace.com/resources-ai. All Insight Exercises and figures are available for download, giving you the flexibility to expand on your reflections and plans.

- **Combine with an App:** While the workbook is great for reflection and thought process, you can use an app for calculations and tracking. If the app doesn't have space for notes, use the workbook to write down your insights and reflections. This dual approach allows you to keep your thoughts organized and accessible.

- **Work Sequentially for Best Results:** It's recommended to go through the workbook one chapter at a time for a structured learning experience. Each chapter builds on the previous one, guiding you through the SEAM framework step-by-step.

- **Feel Free to Explore:** If you're like me, you might want to peek at all the chapters right away. That's okay too! Skim through to get a sense of the whole process, but remember to circle back and complete each chapter thoroughly for the best results.

- **A Semester Course in a Workbook:** With my background teaching at the University of Tennessee at Knoxville and leading training sessions, I've designed this workbook like a semester-long course. Don't be intimidated by that! It's structured to be engaging and interactive, making the learning process enjoyable and practical.

SNAPSHOT:
Evaluating Your Current Career Coordinates

"Curiosity turns uncertainty into discovery."
Madeleine F. Wallace, Ph.D.

The tidal wave of technological change is reshaping industries and careers.

In this new era, simply having competencies is not enough—you need to become a versatilist, someone adaptable and skilled in multiple areas.

But how do you get there? The Snapshot is your crucial first step, serving as a launchpad to gain a clear understanding of your current career situation, including your unique strengths and interests.

The Insight Exercises within the Snapshot provide the self-awareness essential for charting a thriving career path in this ever-evolving landscape. They will help you uncover opportunities you might not have considered before, empowering you to seize control of your future.

The Snapshot has four parts:
PART I: Your Future Readiness
PART II: The Big Three
PART III: Career Development
PART IV: Your Career Profile

IDEA GEM
My Versatilist Journey: The Power of Interdisciplinary Expertise.

Socrates wisely said, "Know thyself." Recognizing and fearlessly applying our unique skills to the work we love helps us pave the way for a fulfilling professional life.

While pursuing my PhD in sociology, I discovered my interest in real-life solutions, which led me to explore multiple disciplines, including engineering. I didn't have a strong background in math, but taking calculus taught me to view problems from unconventional angles and opened my eyes to new ways of modeling social behaviors and interactions. I continued taking courses in other fields outside the typical sociology major's schedule.

This interdisciplinary approach has been key to my success, enabling me to bridge gaps between fields, transfer knowledge seamlessly, and drive innovation. I honed these skills at the NIH and continue to apply them through my consulting company, Windrose Vision, where I assist government agencies, businesses, and nonprofit organizations.

Never be afraid to look beyond your discipline and learn something different.

INFO SNIPPET
The Future of Work: It's All About Your Skills

The job market is rapidly changing, and it's now all about your skills. Companies are moving away from traditional job titles and recognizing that you're a unique individual with diverse talents.

Why It Matters to You:

- **Career Flexibility:** Skills-based hiring expands your career options, allowing you to explore different industries and roles.
- **Adaptability:** Developing in-demand skills future-proofs your career in the face of automation and technological advancements.
- **Personalization:** Knowing your skills helps you tailor your career path to match your strengths and interests.
- **Tailored Responsibilities:** Companies are designing personalized work responsibilities based on your unique skillset.
- **Skills-Based Matching:** Employers are now focused on matching the right skills to the right tasks, ensuring you're in a role where you can truly excel.

SNAPSHOT PART I: YOUR FUTURE READINESS

How well do you know your career self? Whether you're between jobs, considering a career shift, unsure of your next step, or seeking more meaning in your work, understanding your unique skills is essential.

Insight Exercise 1.1 will help you uncover the hidden gems within your skillset— your versatile, transferable skills. This exercise equips you to:

- **Identify your strongest transferable skills:** These are your top assets with the greatest potential across various roles and industries.
- **Understand your average skills:** These skills form a solid foundation, and you could consider further development.
- **Recognize areas for development:** Focus on these to round out your skillset and become more competitive.

INSIGHT EXERCISE 1.1. MY FUTURE-READY SKILLSET

For each future-ready skill in **Table A**, rate your proficiency on a scale of 1 (Poor) to 10 (Excellent). Then, categorize your skills according to your rating:

- **Transferable Skills:** Rated 7 or higher
- **Average Skills:** Rated 5 or 6
- **Areas for Development:** Rated less than 5

Access Fillable PDFs for Insight Exercises at madeleinewallace.com/resources-ai

Table A. Rating and Categorizing My Future-Ready Skills

The Future of Jobs Report 2023 by the World Economic Forum highlights the ten most sought-after, future-ready skills that are essential now and will become increasingly important in the years ahead. This report draws on a comprehensive survey of 803 companies across twenty-seven industry clusters in forty-five different economies, offering a global perspective on skills shaping the future of work (World Economic Forum, 2023).

Future-Ready Skills	Description	How do I rate my proficiency? 1 Poor — 10 Excellent	Categorizing my skills: Transferable (7 or higher) Average (5 or 6) Area for Development (less than 5)
1. Analytical Thinking	Breaking down complex problems into smaller components, examining patterns, and drawing meaningful conclusions. (Ennis, 1996).		
2. Creative Thinking	Thinking innovatively, generating novel ideas, and approaching challenges in unique ways. (Kelley and Kelley, 2013).		
3. Resilience, Flexibility, Agility	Fostering a flexible mindset to prepare for adversity (Coutu 2002), to have the ability to adapt swiftly to change, and to remain stable by pivoting and embracing new ideas. (Denning, 2018).		
4. Motivation	Directing energy towards desired activities with enthusiasm and perseverance with the self-awareness to understand what drives us. (Goleman, 1995).		
5. Curiosity	An unceasing desire to explore, to question, and to understand the world around us both inside and outside the classroom as a lifelong learner. (Leslie, 2014).		

Table A. Rating and Categorizing My Future-Ready Skills (continued)

Future-Ready Skills	Description	How do I rate my proficiency? 1 Poor — 10 Excellent	Categorizing my skills: Transferable (7 or higher) Average (5 or 6) Area for Development (less than 5)
6. Technological Literacy	Knowledge and practical competence applying technology in your chosen field. (Gilster, 1997) and understanding the role of technology in shaping industries, economies, and governance. (Schwab, 2017). An understanding of generative AI[1] and how it creates new and original text, images, music, and simulations using advanced algorithms and neural networks inspired by the human brain. (Stryker and Scapicchio, 2024).		
7. Dependability, Attention to Detail	Consistently producing accurate work of high quality and reliability. (Covey, 1989).		
8. Empathy, Active Listening	Seeing the world through someone else's eyes, with the ability to actively listen to the speaker's message. (Goleman, 2006).		
9. Leadership, Social Influence	Inspiring and motivating others towards a shared vision (Maxwell 1998) with authority, persuasion, social proof, and charisma to guide and to influence others. (Cialdini, 2006).		
10. Quality Control	Ensuring that a product adheres to the highest standards throughout the production cycle. (Deming, 1986).		

[1] Generative AI added by Dr. Madeine F. Wallace to reflect technological landscape at time of publication.

Keep in mind that any assessment captures a snapshot of your skills at a single point in time. The ideal practice is to develop the habit of regularly checking your skills to stay current with industry trends. The market is saturated with tools for assessing personality, career aptitude, and more. Given this variety, refer to the section titled **Choose Wisely: Your Guide to Reliable Skills Assessments** in the Resources page at the end of the chapter. There, you will find a short and easy guide I have developed to help you select additional tools effectively.

SNAPSHOT PART II: THE BIG THREE

Industries are evolving, exploring new directions, and witnessing the emergence of groundbreaking technologies. The arrows in **Figure 1.1** illustrate the cyclical nature of how the Big Three—Relevant Trends, Future Directions, and Emerging Technologies—influence each other and form a continuous loop essential for strategic planning and maintaining a competitive edge in your industry. With this insight, you can identify potential career paths that haven't even been created yet, positioning yourself as a leader who drives innovation and pushes the boundaries of what's possible.

Figure 1.1. The Big Three

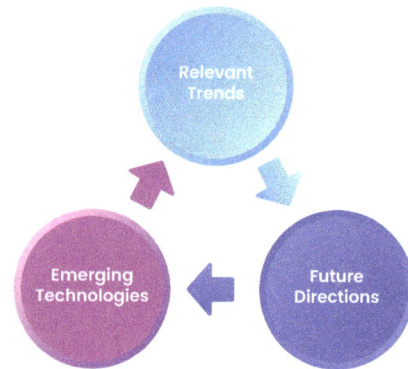

Relevant Trends:
Observable patterns and practices shaping the future of work across different industries. Examples include AI, automation, the gig economy, remote work models, and technology advancements.

Future Directions:
Educated guesses about where the future of work is headed based on current trends, challenges, and potential breakthroughs. Examples include the impact of AI, new business models, and changes in workplace skills.

Emerging Technologies:
New technologies on the horizon (next five to ten years) that have the potential to disrupt various sectors of work. Examples include advanced robotics, blockchain, quantum computing, biotechnologies, renewable energies, and virtual and augmented reality.

> *Relevant trends* **give rise to** *future directions,* **influenced by** *emerging technologies.*
> These emerging technologies drive changes in industry practices and market dynamics.

sonal passions with professional opportunities, enhancing your career satisfaction and setting you up for success. This holistic approach ensures that you are prepared for the future and excited and engaged in your career journey.

The ten future-ready skills are categorized into three buckets of the Big Tree in **Insight Exercise 1.2**

MAPPING YOUR FUTURE-READY SKILLS AND INTEREST WITH THE BIG THREE

Understanding how your skillset fits into the Big Three is crucial for strategically navigating your career and where you want to be. **But what about your personal interests?** It's equally important to assess how your passions intersect with your professional life. By evaluating the relevance of your skills in the context of your personal interests, you can align your per-

- **All Three:** Six skills that are crucial across all contexts.
- **Relevant Trends and Future Directions:** Two skills important for adapting to broader industry trends and leadership roles.
- **Future Directions and Emerging Technologies:** Two skills necessary for staying current with technological advancements.

IDEA GEM
The Drawer Tip

When it's time to do some deep thinking, I institute my **Drawer Tip.** I put my iPhone in the drawer of my desk with an alarm for one hour. As I get immersed in the topic, I change the alarm to 20 minutes to give my eyes a rest from the computer. I never keep my iPhone on my desk when I work; I keep it in the drawer where it cannot distract me from the task at hand! Try it as you work on the Insight Exercises in this workbook!

INSIGHT EXERCISE 1.2. MAPPING MY FUTURE-READY SKILLS WITH THE BIG THREE AND PERSONAL INTERESTS

1. Fill in **My Future-Ready Skills** column in **Table A** with the category you assigned to your skills in **Insight Exercise 1.1**—Transferable, Average, or Area for Development.
2. After labeling your future-ready skills, use the reflection questions in **Table B** to encourage self-awareness, strategic skill development, and alignment of personal interests with professional opportunities. This process will help you brainstorm opportunities that align your interests with your future-ready skills in the evolving job market, whether you aim for a career or your own business.

Table A: My Future-Ready Skills

Big Three Buckets[1]	Future-Ready Skills	My Future-Ready Skills Transferable, Average, or Area for Development
All Three	1. Analytical Thinking	
	2. Creative Thinking	
	4. Motivation	
	7. Dependability, Attention to Detail	
	8. Empathy, Active Listening	
	10. Quality Control	
Relevant Trends and New Directions	3. Resilience, Flexibility, Agility	
	9. Leadership, Social Influence	
New Directions and Emerging Technologies	5. Curiosity	
	6. Technological Literacy	

[1] Refer to **Fitting the Future-Ready Skills in the Big Three Buckets** in the Resources page at the end of the chapter to learn about the rationale behind this categorization.

Table B: Applying My Future-Ready Skills

1. Skill Distribution Balance: Are my "transferable skills" spread evenly across all three Big Buckets?

Insight: *If most of your **transferable skills** are concentrated in just one bucket, consider developing skills in the other buckets to create a more balanced and adaptable skillset. Having all your transferable skills in one bucket and none in the others may indicate a gap in your skillset that needs attention.*

2. Prioritizing Skill Improvement: Where are my "Average" and "Area for Development" skills concentrated?

Insight: *If many of your skills **needing improvement** fall under the "New Directions and Emerging Technologies" category, for instance, prioritize learning opportunities in that area.*

3. Passion Meets Purpose: Beyond my work responsibilities, do I have any hobbies or pursuits that require skills I could also use in my professional setting?

Insight: *This question encourages you to identify hobbies that utilize skills you might not initially consider relevant to your work. However, these skills could be valuable in a professional context, especially if you contemplate shifting to a different industry, sector, or even opening your own business.*

INFO SNIPPET
The Power of the Big Three,
Enablers, and Barriers

As you consider navigating the Big Three in today's dynamic job market, you will encounter enablers and barriers to your goals. Enablers propel you forward toward your goal. Barriers hold you back. Be aware of your enablers and barriers as you master the Big Three.

Enablers:
- **Staying Informed:** Staying updated on the Big Three keeps you aware of market and industry shifts that affect your role.
- **Upskilling and Reskilling:** Knowing when to acquire new skills or enhance existing ones helps you to stay competitive.
- **Maximizing Employability:** Aligning with the Big Three ensures you remain relevant and in demand, particularly in the era of generative AI.

Barriers:
- **Lack of Preparation:** Ignoring the Big Three leaves you unprepared for industry shifts and changing roles.
- **Missed Opportunities for Skill Development:** Failure to upskill or reskill as needed can limit your career growth.
- **Risk of Becoming Obsolete:** Without this knowledge, you risk becoming unemployable or irrelevant in the evolving job market.

INSIGHT EXERCISE 1.3. LEARNING FROM REAL-WORLD SCENARIOS

In **Insight Exercise 1.3,** you will explore the journey of Alex, a program manager who successfully navigated the challenges of digital transformation in the healthcare industry. By examining Alex's experience, you will gain insights into how to proactively enhance your skillset, leverage opportunities, and overcome barriers in your professional development.

1. **Read Alex's Case Study in Figure 1.2:**
   Concentrate on the steps he took to secure his position, enhance his skills, and ultimately lead change within his company.

2. **Reflect on Alex's Journey:**
   Think about how you can apply similar strategies in your current role at work. Consider the objectives and context provided for each question to guide your reflection.

Figure 1.2. Case Study: Alex's Role in Transforming Healthcare through Digital Innovation

Background: Alex, a program manager with a keen interest in technology, found himself at the forefront of healthcare's digital transformation. Faced with uncertainty about his role at a company expanding into remote healthcare, Alex took proactive steps to secure his position. He researched the Big Three—Relevant Trends, Future Directions, and Emerging Technologies—and recorded his conclusions about the industry.

Big Three	Alex's Research Conclusions
Relevant Trends	An increased demand for remote healthcare services means increased regulatory compliance for patient data privacy. This trend underscores the need for robust cybersecurity measures and adherence to new healthcare regulations.
Future Directions	The integration of wearable health tech into patient care will bring challenges in synchronizing operating systems and ensuring seamless data exchange between devices.
Emerging Technologies	The adoption of blockchain for secure patient records exchange will provide high security and bring new regulatory compliance challenges.

Enablers	Barriers
• **Market Demand for Telehealth:** The rising demand for telehealth services propelled the need for technological advancements. • **Acceptance of Change:** Both Alex and the company acknowledged the necessity of change, making it easier to push forward with new initiatives. • **Continuing Education:** Alex's employer sponsored his ongoing education, enabling him to upskill and reskill as needed.	• **Regulatory Compliance:** Meeting new regulations for patient data privacy and security posed significant challenges. • **Synchronization of Technologies:** Ensuring seamless data exchange between wearable health tech and existing systems required substantial effort. • **Potential for Obsolescence:** Without staying informed and adapting to new technologies, the company risked becoming obsolete.

Strategic Actions and Career Decisions

Alex recognized that the company needed to change and acknowledged both the enablers and barriers to technological advancement. He considered his career options and personal circumstances, weighing the possibility of moving to another company already successfully integrating wearable health technology into patient care. However, Alex valued his current job, the company culture, and his colleagues, deciding that he didn't want to leave.
Instead, Alex took the following steps:

1. **Staying Informed:** He kept abreast of the latest relevant trends, future directions, and emerging technologies by continuously researching the Big Three.
2. **Upskilling and Reskilling:** He enrolled in online courses and pursued certifications in advanced healthcare technology, with financial support from his employer.
3. **Maximizing Employability:** By aligning his skills with the Big Three, Alex ensured he remained relevant and in demand.

Alex shared his vision with his boss, proposing a strategic plan to integrate new technology into the company's patient care systems. With added resources from his employer, Alex led the way in successfully implementing these technologies, addressing the regulatory and synchronization challenges head-on.

Outcome

Alex's proactive and strategic approach not only saved the company from potential obsolescence but also earned him a promotion to chief technology officer (CTO) along with a substantial raise. His journey underscores the importance of understanding and leveraging the Big Three to navigate the dynamic job market and achieve career advancement.

INSIGHT EXERCISE 1.3 QUESTIONS

1. Alex researched and upskilled in response to the healthcare industry's digital transformation. Consider the current trends and emerging technologies in your field. **What hot skills or knowledge do you need to acquire to stay relevant?**

2. Alex acknowledged both the market demand for telehealth (an enabler) and the limited expertise in new healthcare technologies at his company (a barrier). He leveraged his company's support to gain additional education and certifications, ultimately leading to a promotion. **What are the enablers and barriers in your current role?**

As you complete **Insight Exercise 1.3,** you might be pondering questions like:

- How can I stay up-to-date on the Big Three?
- How do I learn about and prepare for the potential future directions of my industry?
- What resources can I use to learn about and potentially master emerging technologies?
- How resources do I have to leverage my enablers and remove my barriers?

We will address these questions in Snapshot Part III: Career Development.

**SCIENCE SPOTLIGHT
The Cost of Interruptions**

A 2008 study from the University of California, Irvine, found that interruptions speed up task completion but increase stress and errors, with focus recovery taking about 23 minutes (Mark et al., 2008). Effective attention management minimizes these costs, enhancing productivity and well-being.

This highlights the importance of knowing which career activities are taking your time, allowing you to manage interruptions and boost productivity.

SNAPSHOT PART III: CAREER DEVELOPMENT

Today's professional world is a whirlwind of change. Reaching career goals like growth, maintaining success, and building a strong reputation requires more than just hard work. Strategic and intentional actions are essential. To thrive and to stand out, we need to engage in key activities that build our professional skills, adaptability, and visibility. SEAM offers a menu of career development activities in six key focus areas to ensure success and fulfillment in our careers.

1. **Professional Networking:** Building and leveraging relationships to forge meaningful collaborations and access invaluable industry insights and mentorship.
2. **Staying Informed:** Being aware of industry trends and innovations to stay relevant, competitive, and enable informed decisions.
3. **Practical Application:** Reinforce learning through hands-on experiences so we can handle complex tasks and make visible contributions.
4. **Utilizing Resources:** Enhance skill development to prepare for greater responsibility and career advancement.
5. **Professional Branding:** Establish a professional brand to enhance our identity and credibility.
6. **Educational Career Growth:** Engage in continuous learning by pursuing new degrees, certifications, and specialized training.

Insight Exercise 1.4 offers a list of career development activities to assess your engagement over the last six months.

Insight Exercise 1.5 specifically covers your educational pursuits.

Your answers will shed light on the actions you're taking and highlight areas that require attention.

Access Fillable PDFs for Insight Exercises at madeleinewallace.com/resources-ai

INSIGHT EXERCISE 1.4.
ENGAGEMENT IN CAREER DEVELOPMENT ACTIVITIES

Place a check mark in the column that best describes your engagement for each activity. Check N/A if the activity does not apply to you or to your industry.

In the last six months, how often have you engaged in the following activities?	Not at All	Occasionally	Regularly	N/A
1. Professional Networking				
a. Discuss insights and industry trends with peers to deepen understanding.				
b. Interacted with experts and industry leaders.				
c. Sought advice from mentors.				
d. Worked with a coach for personal development.				
e. Participated in online professional communities.				
f. Spoke at virtual or in-person conference or webinars.				
g. Attended virtual or in-person professional networking events.				
h. Attended university or community-hosted career workshops.				
i. Joined local professional or student organizations field-related				
j. Attended career fairs (early career) or engaged with recruiters (mid-to-advanced careers).				
k. Conducted informational interviews with professionals.				
2. Staying Informed				
a. Explored trends through industry magazines, journals, and reports.				
b. Reviewed insights from industry leaders through blogs, newsletters, email updates, and forecasts.				
c. Listened to industry-related podcasts featuring leaders in the field.				
d. Participated in industry-related meetings, conferences, associations, forums, and webinars.				
e. Viewed industry-related digital channels for video content.				
f. Read industry-related books and e-books to deepen understanding.				
g. Followed industry influencers and thought leaders on social media platforms.				
h. Attended industry expos and trade shows.				
i. Engaged in online discussions and Q&A sessions on platforms, like Reddit or Quora, to gain diverse perspectives.				

INSIGHT EXERCISE 1.4.
ENGAGEMENT IN CAREER DEVELOPMENT ACTIVITIES (CONTINUED)

Place a check mark in the column that best describes your engagement for each activity. Check N/A if the activity does not apply to you or to your industry.

In the last six months, how often have you engaged in the following activities?	Not at All	Occasionally	Regularly	N/A
3. Practical Application				
a. Sought projects or roles that allowed the application of new skills.				
b. Contributed to open-source projects.				
c. Participated in hackathons or innovation challenges.				
d. Implemented new technologies in personal or side projects.				
e. Collaborated on cross-disciplinary projects to apply technical skills in new contexts.				
f. Experimented with emerging technologies through personal projects or trial and error.				
g. Undertook internships or part-time jobs to gain practical experience.				
h. Volunteered for projects or roles in student clubs or organizations.				
i. Engaged in freelance projects or gig work to build experience.				
j. Created and maintained a portfolio of personal projects to demonstrate skills.				
4. Utilizing Resources				
a. Participated in professional development programs.				
b. Participated in leadership development tracks.				
c. Benefited from mentorship or coaching.				
d. Participated in any Employee Resource Groups (ERGs), Business Resource Groups (BRGs), or Affinity Resource Groups (ARGs).				
e. Took part in cross-functional projects.				
f. Experienced job rotations.				
g. Utilized idea incubation funds.				
h. Utilized company-offered online learning platforms and libraries.				
i. Explored different roles through job shadowing.				
j. Participated in boot camps or intensive training programs related to desired industry.				
5. Professional Branding				
a. Updated LinkedIn profile.				
b. Wrote and published articles, blogs, or posts on industry topics.				
c. Contributed to professional online groups and forums.				
d. Optimized online content for better search visibility.				
e. Produced videos, podcasts, and webinars to establish expertise.				
f. Showcased endorsements to enhance credibility.				
g. Created a personal blog or website to share industry-related content and insights.				
h. Participated in online groups or forums to share and receive feedback on professional content.				

INSIGHT EXERCISE 1.5.
EDUCATIONAL CAREER GROWTH

Please respond with Yes or No in the provided spaces.

In the last six months, have you engaged in the following educational endeavors to enhance your technical or future-ready skills?	Technological Skills Yes or No	Future-Ready Skills Yes or No
a. **Engaged in Learning:** Taken courses online or in-person, engaged in self-paced learning modules, and completed industry-relevant massive open online courses (MOOCs).		
b. **Professional Development:** Pursued certifications and attended specialized training workshops.		
c. **Academic Pursuits:** Enrolled in advanced degree programs.		

If you've completed both Insight Exercises, your score is . . . 100%!

Nobody fails these exercises. Their purpose is to encourage honest self-reflection, uncover opportunities for development, discover new career paths, and better prepare for future career advancements.

Next, let's explore your career profile, which will help you determine your path through the next three SEAM steps.

SNAPSHOT PART IV: YOUR CAREER PROFILE

WHAT KIND OF CAREER SEEKER ARE YOU?

As you've journeyed through the Insight Exercises in Snapshot, you've uncovered insights about your professional skills. Now, we invite you to reflect on what you've learned about yourself and select a profile that most closely aligns with your current career stance.

In **Insight Exercise 1.6**, we present seven profiles, ranging from the highly strategic and informed career seekers to those exploring or uncertain about their paths. This spectrum of profiles serves individuals undergoing transitions, those seeking to align their skills better with industry needs, those with a clear vision about their careers, and those in the process of forming one.

While the nature of professional development is complex and dynamic, and you may find that aspects of multiple profiles resonate with you, we ask that you choose the single profile that best represents your current position. This selection is intended to help you focus on your primary career development strategy without confining you to a rigid category.

The profiles are designed to provide guidance and self-reflection, helping you understand your overall approach to career development.

INSIGHT EXERCISE 1.6. DEFINING YOUR PROFESSIONAL PROFILE

Please read the descriptions of the profiles below and add a check mark next to the one that most closely represents you.

Profiles	Vision	Understanding of Industry/Field Trajectory	Skills	I identify myself with . . .
STRATEGIC INNOVATOR	Clear vision aligned with industry demands.	Deep understanding of industry trajectory and demands.	Aware of current skills and development areas for industry alignment.	
SKILLFUL SEEKER	Lacks a clear vision, seeks clarity on career alignment with industry direction.	General understanding of industry's direction, but lacks strategic alignment.	Recognizes skills and knows areas needing development.	
STRATEGIC TRANSITIONER	Transitional vision, seeking new opportunities within or outside current industry based on evolving interests and market trends.	Moderate understanding, focusing on areas with potential for growth or transition.	Identifies core competencies and seeks to expand or adapt skills for new opportunities.	
ADAPTIVE NAVIGATOR	Adaptable, open vision for various industries, recognizing transferable skills.	Broad understanding, adaptable to industry changes	Understands skills and how they can be transferred or adapted.	
ENGAGED LEARNER	Forming vision, focused on acquiring a foundational understanding of the field and its future direction.	Basic understanding of industry trajectory, actively learning.	Has a basic skill set and is aware of areas for growth.	
CURIOUS EXPLORER	Exploratory vision, open to exploring various paths within the industry despite uncertainties about skills	Curious about industry changes but lacks depth of understanding.	Unclear about skills and areas of development.	
UNCERTAIN VOYAGER	Unclear vision, disengaged and uncertain about future direction.	Limited understanding of industry and personal career trajectory.	Unclear about skills to develop or focus on.	

Congratulations! By completing your Snapshot, you've gained valuable insights about yourself and selected a profile to help reshape the trajectory of your career using this workbook. Your journey continues with the Envision step, where you will learn how to create a flexible future, explore new possibilities, and set essential goals to achieve your career aspirations.

Discover the challenges for each profile by scanning the QR code or visiting madeleinewallace.com/resources-ai to download exclusive content.

**Access Fillable PDFs for
Insight Exercises at
madeleinewallace.com/resources-ai**

LEARNING LOCK-IN

Beyond identifying your strengths and areas for development to remain competitive and relevant, **what new insights have you gained about yourself from engaging with the Insight Exercises in the SEAM Snapshot?**

Chapter 1: Resources

Choose Wisely: Your Guide to Reliable Skills Assessments

For a deeper dive into your skills beyond your self-reflection, take one of the existing skills assessments on the market. Skills and personality assessments can provide surprising insights into your strengths and weaknesses in the workplace. If some of the better-known ones (Myers-Briggs, DISC, StrengthFinders, etc.) are out of reach, you may be tempted to do a lesser-known, free assessment. There are many online. If you go this route, the chart below will help you make a good choice. It outlines what you should look for to ensure that your assessment will be based in science, unbiased, and yield trustworthy, usable results.

Criteria	Application to Career Development Resources	Application to Self-Assessment Tools	Check (✓)
Source Authority and Expertise	Does the source have a strong reputation and relevant expertise in your industry?	Is the tool developed or endorsed by reputable organizations or professionals in career counseling or psychological assessments?	
Evidence-Based Information	Is the advice backed by research, data, or proven success stories?	Is the tool based on well-researched career development theories or personality assessment models?	
Relevance	Is the content up-to-date and in sync with current industry standards and trends?	Is the tool regularly reviewed and revised to reflect the latest research and labor market trends?	
Objective and Unbiased	Is the information presented without a sales pitch, focusing on genuine advice?	Does the tool provide results and career suggestions objectively, without financial bias towards specific paths?	
User Reviews or Expert Endorsement	Are there positive testimonials from users or endorsements from industry experts?	Are there positive reviews from users who found the tool helpful, or do professionals recommend it?	

Fitting the Future-Ready Skills in the Big Three Buckets

Future-Ready Skill	Big Three Buckets	Why It Belongs in the Bucket
Analytical Thinking	All Three	Strong analytical skills are crucial for understanding complex trends, problem-solving in a changing work environment, and adapting to new technologies.
Creative Thinking	All Three	Creativity is essential for finding innovative solutions, developing new business models, and adapting to unforeseen challenges in the future of work.
Resilience, Flexibility and Agility	Relevant Trends, Future Directions	These skills are increasingly valuable in a dynamic work environment with evolving trends and potential job disruptions.
Motivation and Self-Awareness	All Three	Understanding your strengths and weaknesses and maintaining motivation are key for lifelong learning and adapting to the demands of future work.
Curiosity and Lifelong Learning	Future Directions, Emerging Technologies	A curious mindset and willingness to learn continuously are essential for keeping up with advancements and thriving in a rapidly changing work landscape.
Technological Literacy	Future Directions, Emerging Technologies	Basic to advanced technological literacy becomes increasingly important as new technologies emerge and influence work processes.
Dependability and Attention to Detail	All Three	These skills remain valuable across different work environments and are essential for maintaining quality and delivering results.
Empathy and Active Listening	All Three	Effective communication and building strong relationships are crucial for teamwork, collaboration, and navigating diverse work settings.
Leadership and Social Influence	Relevant Trends, Future Directions	Leadership skills, even in non-traditional roles, can be valuable for collaboration, team motivation, and navigating new work models that may emphasize project-based work.
Quality Control	All Three	Maintaining high-quality work remains important regardless of future trends. However, the methods and tools for quality control may evolve with new technologies.

Chapter 2

ENVISION:
Building a
Flexible Future

"Design your future by building
it today."
Madeleine F. Wallace, Ph.D.

n your Snapshot, you identified the profile that most accurately illustrates where you are in your career journey. Building on that foundation, the Envision step equips you to move beyond the present and visualizes your future career within a changing world.

Your Envision step has five parts:
PART I: Exploration Sprint
PART II: Charting Your Course
PART III: Exploring Career Scenarios
PART IV: Creating a Career Vision
PART V: Setting Flexible and Fixed Goals

Exploration Sprints

**INFO SNIPPET
SEAM Exploration Sprints**

SEAM Exploration Sprints offer several benefits:

- **Focused Learning** → Short, intense learning periods reduce distractions and speed up skilling.
- **Feedback and Iteration** → Ensures continuous learning by allowing shifts to other areas and promoting ongoing improvement.
- **Risk Mitigation** → Provides a safe space for exploring new skills and minimizing long-term risks.
- **Enhanced Self-Awareness** → Encourages exploration, fostering improved career decisions through regular reflection and adaptability.

ENVISION PART I: EXPLORATION SPRINT

Traditional methods urge you to define your career vision first, but as we learned in the Insight Exercises in the Snapshot step, you may not be ready to do that yet. You may need more information and perspectives to inform your career path.

SEAM offers a personalized and targeted experience called the **Exploration Sprint.** Inspired by Agile Methodology (Cohn, 2005), an **Exploration Sprint** is an actionable and time-bound, two-to-six-week activity designed to help you:

- Explore your current or target industry
- Sample essential skills required for various careers
- Uncover new interests

BEFORE, DURING, AND AFTER YOUR EXPLORATION SPRINT

An **Exploration Sprint** will help you understand the Big Three within your field or industry—Relevant Trends, Future Directions, and Emerging Technologies. Since most of us don't know everything there is to know about the future soon to impact our careers, we must educate ourselves by purposefully planning our Exploration Sprints.

Your career profile can provide guidance as to the best activities to choose for your sprint. **Figure 2.1** offers some suggestions based on your chosen profile.

Figure 2.1. Exploration Sprint Activities by Career Profile

Profile	Activity (Key Focus Area[1])	Potential for Exploratory Sprint
STRATEGIC INNOVATOR	a. Discuss insights from your reading with professional peers to gain further understanding. (Professional Networking)	
	b. Review insights from industry leaders through blogs, newsletters, email updates, and forecasts. (Staying Informed)	
	c. Participate in hackathons or innovation challenges. (Practical Application)	
	d. Utilize idea incubation funds. (Utilizing Resources)	
	e. Produce videos, podcasts, and webinars to establish expertise. (Professional Branding)	
	a. Engage in Learning: Take courses online or in-person, engage in self-paced learning modules, and complete industry-relevant MOOCs. (Educational Career Growth)	
	[2] Other:_____	
SKILLFUL SEEKER	b. Interact with experts and industry leaders. (Professional Networking)	
	a. Explore trends through industry magazines, journals, and reports. (Staying Informed)	
	g. Undertake internships or part-time jobs to gain practical experience. (Practical Application)	
	j. Participate in boot camps or intensive training programs related to desired industry. (Utilizing Resources)	
	h. Participate in online groups or forums to share and receive feedback on professional content. (Professional Branding)	
	b. Professional Development: Pursue certifications and attend specialized training workshops. (Educational Career Growth)	
	Other: _____	

[1] Each activity is aligned with and belongs to a specific key focus area, as outlined in Insight Exercise 1.4 of the Snapshot Step.

[2] "Other" enables personalized exploration with activities beyond the key focus areas.

Figure 2.1. Exploration Sprint Activities by Career Profile (continued)

Profile	Activity (Key Focus Area)	Potential for Exploratory Sprint
STRATEGIC TRANSITIONER	c. Seek advice from mentors. (Utilizing Resources)	
	d. Participate in industry-related meetings, conferences, associations, forums, and webinars. (Staying Informed)	
	e. Collaborate on cross-disciplinary projects to apply technical skills in new contexts. (Practical Application)	
	f. Experience job rotations. (Utilizing Resources)	
	g. Follow industry influencers and thought leaders on social media platforms. (Staying Informed)	
	c. Academic Pursuits: Enroll in advanced degree programs. (Educational Career Growth)	
	Other: _____	
ADAPTIVE NAVIGATOR	d. Work with a coach for personal development. (Professional Networking)	
	e. View industry-related YouTube channels for video content. (Staying Informed)	
	h. Volunteer for projects or roles in student clubs or organizations. (Utilizing Resources)	
	i. Explore different roles through job shadowing. (Utilizing Resources)	
	i. Engage in online discussions and Q&A sessions on platforms to gain diverse perspectives. (Staying Informed)	
	a. Engage in Learning: Take courses online or in-person, engaged in self-paced learning modules, and completed industry-relevant MOOCs. (Educational Career Growth)	
	Other: _____	

Figure 2.1. Exploration Sprint Activities by Career Profile (continued)

Profile	Activity (Key Focus Area)	Potential for Exploratory Sprint
ENGAGED LEARNER	g. Attend virtual or in-person professional networking events. (Professional Networking)	
	f. Read industry-related books and e-books to deepen understanding. (Staying Informed)	
	g. Experiment with emerging technologies through personal projects or trial and error. (Practical Application)	
	a. Participate in professional development programs. (Educational Career Growth)	
	j. Conduct informational interviews with professionals. (Professional Networking)	
	b. Professional Development: Pursue certifications and attended specialized training workshops. (Educational Career Growth)	
	Other: _____	
CURIOUS EXPLORER	h. Attend university or community-hosted career workshops. (Professional Networking)	
	h. Utilize company-offered online learning platforms and libraries. (Utilizing Resources)	
	i. Engage in freelance projects or gig work to build experience. (Practical Application)	
	b. Write and publish articles, blogs, or posts on industry topics. (Professional Branding)	
	f. Read Industry-related books and e-books to deepen understanding. (Staying Informed)	
	a. Engage in Learning: Take courses online or in-person, engage in self-paced learning modules, and complete industry-relevant MOOCs. (Educational Career Growth)	
	Other: _____	

Figure 2.1. Exploration Sprint Activities by Career Profile (continued)

Profile	Activity (Key Focus Area)	Potential for Exploratory Sprint
UNCERTAIN VOYAGER	h. Volunteer for projects or roles in student clubs or organizations. (Practical Application)	
	i. Join local professional, or student organizations related to your field. (Professional Networking)	
	c. Seek advice from mentors, colleagues, former managers. (Utilizing Resources)	
	h. Attend industry expos and trade shows. (Staying Informed)	
	k. Conduct informational interviews with professionals. (Professional Networking)	
	a. Engage in Learning: Take courses online or in-person, engage in self-paced learning modules, and complete industry-relevant MOOCs. (Educational Career Growth)	
	Other: _____	

IDEA GEM
Breaking Inertia: Using SEAM Exploration Sprints to Discover Your Career Path

According to Newton's law of inertia, a body at rest will stay at rest unless acted upon by an external force. Similarly, your future self will remain unchanged and inactive unless you apply an external force. In SEAM, the "exploration sprints" are the external forces you engage in to initiate action in your career. These sprint activities are part of a broader strategy to help you discover your interests. By actively committing to these sprints, you break the inertia, propelling your future self toward growth and achievement.

INSIGHT EXERCISE 2.1. PLANNING AND EXECUTING MY EXPLORATION SPRINTS

In this exercise, you'll complete two exploration sprints, documenting your reflections before, during, and after each one. Each sprint should last two to six weeks and can be done consecutively or concurrently

1. **Locate Your Profile:** Locate your profile in **Figure 2.1** (e.g., Strategic Innovator). This figure lists activities for exploratory sprints, organized by profile. Each activity includes its Key Focus Area in parentheses.

2. **Evaluate Each Activity for Sprint Potential:** Use the blank column titled "Potential for Exploratory Sprint" to record whether each activity is a good candidate for a sprint. Cross-reference each activity in **Figure 2.1** with **Exercise 1.4** and assess its potential:
   - If you rated an activity as **"not at all"** or **"occasionally,"** mark it as a candidate for your sprint.
   - If you rated it **"regularly,"** it's likely not a priority for your sprint.

Example

If you have the "Strategic Innovator" profile, review each activity. For instance, look at activity "c. Participate in hackathons or innovation challenges (Practical Application)," and check it in **Exercise 1.4.** If it's rated **"not at all"** or **"occasionally,"** mark it as a sprint candidate in the blank column titled "Potential for Exploratory Sprint."

3. **Select Your Sprint Activities:** Review your list of potential sprint candidates in the final column and select two activities that you'll focus on for **Exploration Sprint 1** and **Exploration Sprint 2.**

4. **Document Your Exploration Sprint:** After selecting your two sprint activities, use the **"My Exploration Sprint"** form to fill in the basic details (Sprint Number, Start Date, and End Date) and complete the reflection questions.

My Exploration Sprint #: _____ **Career Profile:** _____

List Activity from Figure 2.1.

- Activity Start Date (MM/DD/YYYY): ____ / ____ / ____   Activity End Date:(MM/DD/YYYY): ____ / ____ / ____
- What specific tasks do you plan to do as part of the activity you selected for your exploration sprint?

_____

_____

Pre-Exploration Sprint Reflection (To be completed upon selecting an activity and before starting it.)

- Pre-Exploration Date (MM/DD/YYYY): ____ / ____ / ____
- How will this activity benefit your career exploration or work?

_____

_____

Mid-Exploration Sprint Reflection (To be completed at the mid-point of the sprint.)

- Mid-Exploration Date (MM/DD/YYYY): ____ / ____ / ____
- How can you apply what you are learning to real-world scenarios or projects?

_____

_____

Post-Exploration Sprint Reflection (To be completed as soon as possible after the sprint ends.)

- Post-Exploration Date (MM/DD/YYYY): ____ / ____ / ____
- What was the biggest challenge you encountered in completing this sprint? (e.g., time management, lack of resources)

_____

_____

- What new interests or career paths did the activity spark that you might want to explore further?

_____

_____

- What kind of support system (e.g., mentor, networking group) would be most beneficial for you moving forward to learn more about this topic?

_____

_____

**Download fillable PDFs for additional Exploration Sprints (Insight Exercise 2.1) at
madeleinewallace.com/resources-ai.**

IDEA GEM
Breaking Free from the Box

Imagine your career as a box. At first glance, it might seem confining, with rigid walls limiting your movement. But within this box, there's room to grow. You can move forward, backward, and sideways, exploring every inch of your potential.

For me, this box represented my experience while pursuing my master's and PhD. U.S. immigration laws for international students didn't allow me to work outside the university, but within these constraints, I discovered numerous opportunities. While completing the required coursework, I also took extra courses without additional cost in engineering, business, statistics, political science, ecology, public health, and exercise science. Thanks to my teaching/research assistantship, I was able to push the boundaries of my box and explore these diverse fields.

Each step within the box added to my growth. The more I explored, the more I learned, and the stronger I became. One day, I realized that the box wasn't as confining as it seemed. I had created opportunities within it that eventually allowed me to break free.

Today, exposure to diverse fields has opened countless doors for me. I've worked in various industries, bringing a unique blend of knowledge and skills. The box that once seemed limiting became the foundation for my expansive career.

When you feel confined in your career, remember that there's always room to grow within your box. Explore every direction, learn as much as you can, and use your experiences to build strength. One day, you'll find a way to open the box, jump higher, push harder, or have someone open it for you.

Today's constraints are tomorrow's stepping stones to success!

ENVISION PART II: CHARTING YOUR COURSE

DO NOT DO THIS PART OF THE ENVISION STEP UNTIL YOU HAVE COMPLETED YOUR EXPLORATION SPRINTS.

A FOUNDATION FOR A CAREER VISION

Before we dive into creating your career vision, it's essential to first understand the environment in which you'll be navigating. Today's career pathways demand continuous self-reflection and the flexibility to adjust strategies to remain relevant and resilient. By thoroughly understanding the landscape, you can craft a more informed and achievable career vision.

CHALLENGES FROM EXTERNAL FACTORS

External factors can present significant challenges, potentially hindering your advancement within your current industry, transitioning to new industries, or pivoting into a completely new career direction. Recognizing these challenges is crucial as it enables you to strategically invest your time, energy, and resources in areas with the highest potential for success.

Insight Exercise 2.2 explores these external factors and their potential impacts on your career. Be sure to add any external factors you identify that are not listed, ensuring your chart is comprehensive and tailored to your unique situation.

Understanding your environment is a critical step toward crafting a meaningful and realistic career vision. Let's explore these external factors together and lay a solid foundation for your future career aspirations.

INSIGHT EXERCISE 2.2.
IMPACT OF POTENTIAL EXTERNAL CHALLENGES

Reflect on how external factors are presenting potential negative challenges for your career. Rate the perceived negative impact high, medium, low, or none.

External Factors	Potential Challenges	Perceived Negative Impact High, Medium, Low, or None
1. Economic Conditions	Recessions, unemployment rates, or industry downturns.	
2. Technological Changes	Rapid advancements that make certain skills obsolete.	
3. Market Demand	Fluctuations in the demand for specific roles or industries.	
4. Regulatory Changes	Laws and regulations that impact industry practices.	
5. Competition	High competition for desired roles or career paths.	
6. Educational Opportunities	Availability and accessibility of upskilling and reskilling programs	
7. Corporate Culture	Organizational environments that may not align with individual growth.	
8. Networking Opportunities	Limited access to professional networks or mentors.	
9. Globalization	International competition and opportunities affecting local career prospects.	
10. Other: _____	Other: _____	

NAVIGATING PERSONAL CIRCUMSTANCES FOR CAREER STRENGTH

Personal circumstances—such as family commitments, financial needs, and health issues—can have a profound impact on your career trajectory.

By understanding how these factors influence your professional life, you can better shape your career development strategies. Recognizing the role of personal circumstances allows you to identify new opportunities, set realistic career goals, and determine when to make pivotal changes. This awareness also helps you create proactive plans to overcome challenges and leverage your circumstances for career advancement.

INSIGHT EXERCISE 2.3. IMPACT OF PERSONAL CIRCUMSTANCES

In this exercise, you will reflect on how various personal circumstances might be affecting your career development. The bullet points under each challenge description serve as prompts to guide your thinking as you assess and rate the negative impact of each circumstance. Your task is to evaluate how strongly each factor influences your career (high, medium, low, or none) and record your rating in the third column.

Personal Circumstances	Challenge Description	Negative Impact High, Medium, Low, or None
1. Financial Limitations	Insufficient funds to pursue upskilling or reskilling programs. • Does my financial situation impact my ability to reskill and upskill? • Can I do anything about it?	
2. Family Responsibilities	Commitments to caregiving that limit time and mobility. • How do my family commitments affect my career choices and opportunities?	
3. Health Issues	Physical or mental health challenges that affect work capacity. • Do my physical or mental health challenges influence my work capacity and career progress? • Is there anything more I can do to effectively manage my health issues?	
4. Skill Gaps	Lack of necessary skills or difficulty acquiring new ones. • Is my career being held back by a lack of skills? • Are there obstacles to developing the skills I need?	
5. Lack of Confidence	Self-doubt in abilities to pursue or achieve career goals. • Does self-doubt impact my ability to pursue or achieve career goals? • Can I take action to build your confidence and self-belief?	
6. Risk Aversion	Fear of failure or reluctance to leave a stable job for uncertain opportunities. • Does my fear of failure or reluctance to leave a stable job affect my career decisions? • What strategies can I adopt to manage risks and embrace new opportunities?	
7. Personal Values	Career choices that may conflict with personal beliefs or values • Is it limiting to find an organization whose values align with mine?	
8. Work-Life Balance Priorities	Desire for a balanced lifestyle that may limit career choices. • Do I need flexibility in my schedule? • Do I need to have set hours?	
9. Geographical Constraints	Location limitations that affect job opportunities. • Am I willing and able to relocate for the right job opportunity?	
10. Other: _____	Other:	

ENVISION PART III: EXPLORING CAREER PREPAREDNESS SCENARIOS

Being prepared for change is the key to thriving in today's dynamic world. Scenario planning empowers you to anticipate a range of possibilities, building unshakeable career resilience and the agility to pivot with confidence as circumstances evolve.

You will now develop three career scenarios—best case, worst case, and balanced—as part of **Insight Exercise 2.4. Career Preparedness Scenario Strategies.**

Figure 2.2 defines each scenario and provides four key questions to guide your scenario development. It also includes an example illustrating how to use your negative impact ratings from Part II, along with your responses to the key questions, to craft your scenarios. Each question is designed to help you gain valuable insights into your career adaptability and refine your strategies for navigating any situation with confidence.

Figure 2.2. Question Bank for Insight Exercise 2.4

A. Career Scenarios

- **Best-Case Scenario:** External factors and personal circumstances align to create the most favorable realistic career outcome. This scenario represents an optimal outcome.
- **Worst-Case Scenario:** Challenging external factors and personal circumstances combine to present the most difficult scenario you could realistically face. This exercise is strategic, helping you prepare for the unexpected.
- **Balanced Scenario:** A combination of external factors and personal circumstances presents a moderately challenging, yet manageable, situation. Balanced scenarios address current trends and likely events.

B. Key Questions

Q1: What roles and activities are you engaging in for this scenario? Are they focused on leadership, teamwork, creative problem-solving, or technical expertise?
Purpose: To identify the nature of these roles and clarify the work environment and tasks that motivate you and contribute to your professional fulfillment.

Q2: Are your roles and activities strategic, operational, technical, or social?
Purpose: To understand which types of challenges engage you most and align with your skills and passions.

Q3: Who benefits from your work in this scenario? Are you helping a specific group of people, a community, an industry, or a global cause?
Purpose: To reveal your values and the broader purpose that drives your career choices.

Q4: How do you feel about the work you're doing in this scenario? Do you feel challenged, satisfied, stressed, or joyful?
Purpose: To gauge your emotional response and gain insight into potential job satisfaction and work-life integration.

Figure 2.2. Question Bank for Insight Exercise 2.4 (continued)

C. Example Scenario Development

Mary, a cybersecurity professional, wants to determine her best-case career scenario. In **Insight Exercise 2.2**, she rated Market Demand as having a **low negative impact** because her skills are in high demand. Similarly, in **Insight Exercise 2.3**, she rated Risk Aversion as having a **low negative impact** because she is a courageous risk-taker.

Mary answers the questions in Section B to create her best-case scenario based on this low negative impact information.

Career Preparedness Best-Case Scenario

Select and record one **LOW negative impact** area from:
- **Insight Exercise 2.2 (external circumstances):** Market Demand
- **Insight Exercise 2.3 (personal circumstances):** Risk Aversion.

Q1: I have been keeping up with developments in my field and want to work as part of a team, possibly in a leadership role. I am the senior member of my team and have exhibited the ability to be a leader.

Q2: I have a great deal of technical expertise but also enjoy strategic work, like working on the programming for the solutions we create.

Q3: I want to be involved at a higher level of cybersecurity to serve the federal government and, by extension, everyone in the country. Professionals like me are in great demand in Washington, D.C.

Q4: I find cybersecurity rewarding and challenging. I believe my work is important and can impact millions, which is what I want to do. I would like a hybrid environment, as I have young children at home.

Best-Case Scenario Description (write in present tense): I secure a government cybersecurity position, potentially requiring relocation to Washington, D.C. The role is more satisfying and lucrative than my current position, and I lead a small team on a larger project. The position offers a hybrid work environment, allowing me flexibility to manage my responsibilities at home.

INSIGHT EXERCISE 2.4.
CAREER PREPAREDNESS SCENARIO STRATEGIES

1. **Describe** your best, worst, and balanced career scenarios using the work you have done in **Insight Exercises 2.2 (Impact of External Challenges)** and **2.3 (Impact of Personal Circumstances)**. Select the specific challenges and circumstances that you perceive have the most significant impact on your career.

2. **Review** the information and example in **Figure 2.2**, "Question Bank for **Insight Exercise 2.4.**"

3. **For each scenario**, answer the key questions listed in **Figure 2.2** to help you develop a clear understanding of your best, worst, and balanced career scenarios.

• **Career Preparedness Best-Case Scenario**

a. Create a scenario using the external factors and personal circumstances that you rated as having a LOW negative impact.

Example: If you rated Market Demand (an external factor) as having a LOW negative impact due to the high demand for your skills, and Risk Aversion (a personal circumstance) as LOW negative impact because you are a risk-taker, use these to frame your best-case scenario. (Refer to the example at the bottom of **Figure 2.2** for guidance on how to describe your best-case scenario.)

b. Select and record one **LOW negative impact** area from each of the following:

- Insight Exercise 2.2 (external circumstances): _____
- Insight Exercise 2.3 (personal circumstances): _____

c. **Answer** the **four key questions from Figure 2.2** to develop your best-case career scenario:

Response Q1: _____
Response Q2: _____
Response Q3: _____
Response Q4: _____

d. **Describe your Best-Case Scenario** using the responses you provided to the key questions (write in present tense):

_____

_____

_____

• **Career Preparedness Worst-Case Scenario**

b. Create a scenario using the external factors and personal circumstances that you rated as having a HIGH negative impact. Envision the path your career could take at the intersection of these two unfavorable circumstances.

Example: If you rated Regulatory Changes (an external factor) as having a HIGH negative impact due to threats to your industry, and Family Responsibilities (a personal circumstance) as HIGH negative impact because your child requires increasing at-home care, use these to frame your worst-case scenario.

b. Select and record one **HIGH negative impact** area from each of the following:
- Insight Exercise 2.2 (external circumstances): _____
- Insight Exercise 2.3 (personal circumstances): _____

c. Answer the **four key questions from Figure 2.2** to develop your worst-case career scenario:

Response to Q1: _____
Response to Q2: _____
Response to Q3: _____
Response to Q4: _____

d.   **Describe your Worst-Case Scenario** using the responses you provided to the key questions (write in present tense):

_____

_____

_____

• Career Preparedness Balanced Scenario

c.   Create a scenario using the external factors and personal circumstances that you rated as having a **MEDIUM negative impact.** This scenario should reflect a moderately challenging situation that is manageable but requires careful navigation.

Example: If you rated Corporate Culture (an external factor) as having a MEDIUM negative impact because changes are needed in your organization, and Personal Values (a personal circumstance) as MEDIUM negative impact because the company aligns with some, but not all, of your personal values, use these to frame your balanced scenario.

b.   Select and record one **MEDIUM negative impact** area from each of the following:

   • Insight Exercise 2.2 (external circumstances): _____
   • Insight Exercise 2.3 (personal circumstances): _____

c.   Answer the **four key questions from Figure 2.2** to develop your balanced career scenario:

   Response to Q1: _____
   Response to Q2: _____
   Response to Q3: _____
   Response to Q4: _____

d.   **Describe your Balanced Scenario** using the responses you provided to the key questions (write in present tense):

_____

_____

_____

What revelations do you have from developing different futures for your career?

_____

_____

_____

_____

ENVISION PART IV: CREATING A CAREER VISION

In Part III, you developed best, worst, and balanced career scenarios to prepare for various possibilities in your professional journey. These hypothetical scenarios were designed to help you think about potential challenges and opportunities, fostering a mindset of resilience and adaptability.

Now, it's time to leverage the insights gained from these scenarios to help shape your career vision. Rather than viewing your career vision as a fixed destination, consider it a guiding compass that will help you navigate the complexities of your professional life, supporting a resilient and fulfilling career journey.

Your career vision should:
- **Be Informed by the Broader Context of the Big Three:** Consider insights from relevant trends, future directions, and emerging technologies that will shape the future of work.
  - *Reflective Question:* What path do I see myself on based on current relevant trends and emerging technologies?

- **Be Grounded in Reality:** Acknowledge life's external pressures, including potential challenges and unique personal circumstances.
  - *Reflective Question:* What personal circumstances or challenges should I consider when planning my career?
- **Be Attainable:** Be possible to achieve with the resources and time available, even when obstacles arise.
  - *Reflective Question:* What resources and time constraints do I need to consider?
- **Prioritize Well-Being:** Consider your physical, mental, and emotional health as integral to your career success.
  - *Reflective Question:* What aspects of my career support my physical, mental, and emotional well-being, and how can I incorporate more of these elements into my career vision?
- **Be Personally Fulfilling and Professionally Satisfying:** Strive for a balance that brings both personal joy and professional accomplishment.
  - *Reflective Question:* What aspects of my career bring me joy and fulfillment, and how can I incorporate more of these elements into my career vision?

Your career vision will evolve as you grow and as the world changes around you. Technological advancements, shifting industry landscapes, and personal development all contribute to this dynamic process. Being adaptable and open to revising your vision will help you stay aligned with your goals and values over time.

**IDEA GEM
THE WINDROSE NAME**

Windrose ✦ Vision

I named my company Windrose because the wind rose, the predecessor of the compass, was a vital tool sailors once used to navigate uncharted waters. Just as the wind rose provided direction and guidance for ancient mariners, developing a clear career vision is essential to navigate the complexities of your professional journey. Your career vision acts as your true north, giving you a sense of purpose and direction. By identifying what you aspire to achieve and how you want to grow, you set the foundation for making intentional choices that guide you toward your goals while remaining adaptable to changes and opportunities that come from all directions.

FLEXIBLE VERSUS FIXED CAREER VISIONS

A **Flexible** Career Vision
- Embraces change within an unpredictable job market
- Fosters adaptability and a positive response to change
- Evolves over time to remain relevant and fulfilling despite personal and professional shifts
- Leverages opportunities for growth

A **Fixed** Career Vision
- Provides a clear, stable target
- Focuses on achieving specific professional milestones, roles, or achievements
- Requires frequent analysis and revision to stay relevant

Figure 2.3 gives examples for flexible and fixed career vision. SEAM advocates for a flexible career vision with a responsive approach to career planning. Flexibility allows you to proactively navigate your career and take control of your future.

However, the choice between a flexible or fixed career vision ultimately depends on your circumstances. Understanding the nuances between the two types of career visions is crucial for making informed decisions about your career path.

Figure 2.3. Flexible Versus Fixed Career Vision Examples

My passion lies in crafting compelling marketing strategies that resonate with diverse audiences. I'll experiment with different channels like social media, content marketing, and email marketing, constantly analyzing data to optimize campaigns and to refine my approach. I'm open to exploring various marketing specializations or industries, allowing me to tailor my skills to a niche market and identify the best fit for my talents.

**Flexible
Career Vision
Marketing Specialist**

I envision myself as a director of digital marketing in the supermarket industry, focusing on the organic and health-conscious retail sector. My goal is to master social media marketing principles and best practices tailored specifically for this industry. I plan to build a strong portfolio showcasing successful campaigns for relevant brands, with the aim of landing a marketing position at Whole Foods. I want to create impactful marketing solutions that meet business objectives while also catering to the needs of health-conscious customers.

**Fixed
Career Vision
Marketing Specialist**

Figure 2.3. Flexible Versus Fixed Career Vision Examples (continued)

My mission is to make a positive impact on students' lives, fostering a love for learning through adaptable teaching methods. I'll continuously explore and refine my approach, tailoring it to diverse learning styles and classroom dynamics. I'm open to opportunities in various grade levels and subject areas, ultimately aiming to find the environment where I can best utilize my skills and passion for education. In the future, I may even pursue leadership roles or focus on curriculum development to contribute to broader educational improvements.

**Flexible
Career Vision
Educator**

My vision is to become a dedicated high school-level teacher in history. I'll pursue the necessary degrees and certification and gain experience in my chosen subject area, focusing on developing effective teaching strategies for my students. This path will ensure I achieve my vision to contribute to the success of high school students in learning history within a specific educational setting.

**Fixed
Career Vision
Educator**

INSIGHT EXERCISE 2.5.
CAREER VISION

Reflect on your aspirations and the insights gained from previous exercises to articulate your career vision. Determine whether your vision will be flexible or fixed.

MY CAREER VISION   **Flexible**_____ **Fixed**_____

_____

_____

_____

GATHERING CONSTRUCTIVE FEEDBACK

Your next step is to seek feedback from someone significant in your professional life, such as a mentor, supervisor, or colleague. This feedback is valuable for determining whether your career statement is realistic and accurately reflects your potential. Consider the following sources for valuable insights:

- **Manager or Team Leader:** They have insights into your capabilities, work ethic, and professional growth. They also have a valuable perspective on the organization and the impact you can make internally.
- **Colleague:** A trusted coworker has a close-up viewpoint of your team collaboration skills, dependability, and day-to-day contributions.
- **Mentor or Industry Expert:** They have extensive experience and can offer valuable perspectives on industry trends and future opportunities.
- **Team member:** Feedback from a member of the team that you lead can offer insights into your leadership style and effectiveness.
- **Stakeholder:** A client or a recipient of your organization's services can offer input on your communication style and engagement.

Choose individuals for career feedback who know you well enough to provide meaningful insights into your career vision. Selecting people from diverse roles will give you a range of perspectives. First, identify the specific feedback you need, which will help you choose the most appropriate person to propel your career development. For more information on soliciting feedback during your career journey, see **All About Feedback** in the Resources section at the end of the chapter.

INSIGHT EXERCISE 2.6.
GATHERING FEEDBACK

Share your career vision with someone appropriate who knows you well on a professional level. Ask them if they feel your statement is achievable and accurately reflects a healthy opportunity to maximize your potential. Then, complete a revised career vision based on their feedback.

Commenter's Name: _____

Commenter's Title: _____

Commenter's Feedback: _____

_____

_____

REVISED CAREER VISION BASED ON FEEDBACK:

_____

_____

_____

SCIENCE SPOTLIGHT
Writing Down Goals

A study by a Dominican University professor found that writing down goals and sharing progress boosts success (Matthews, 2007).

Here are the key findings:
- People who wrote down their goals were 42 % more likely to succeed compared to those who did not.
- People who sent weekly updates to a friend achieved their goals over 70 % of the time, in contrast to only 35 % of those who kept their goals private and did not document them.

Start today—write down your goals and take the first step toward achieving them!

ENVISION PART V: SETTING FLEXIBLE AND FIXED GOALS

It's time to set goals with your vision statement in mind. Setting clear, well-defined goals is crucial to achieving your career vision. Goals act as milestones on your career journey, guiding your actions and providing a sense of direction and purpose.

STEPS FOR SETTING SEAM GOALS

1. **Review Your Vision:** Your goals should be directly generated from your career vision statement. This approach ensures that every step you take moves you closer to realizing your vision, maintaining consistency and coherence in your career path.

2. **Identify Key Themes and Determine Sequence:** Look for recurring themes or major objectives that stand out in your vision statement. These themes will form the foundation of your goals. Then, determine which goals should be tackled first. Some goals will naturally follow one another in sequence, while others may be pursued concurrently.

3. **Categorize Goals into Flexible or Fixed:** A fixed career vision can have flexible goals, and a flexible career vision can have fixed goals. Even with a clear, stable career target outlined in a fixed career vision, the steps you take to get there can adapt to changing circumstances (flexible goals). Conversely, if your career vision is more adaptable (flexible career vision), you can set specific, unchanging goals (fixed goals) to anchor your progress.

Examples:

- **Figure 2.4:** This figure shows the three distinct goals drawn from a flexible career vision statement for a marketing specialist. Notice how the different themes of the vision are underlined and then reworded to become goals.

Figure 2.4. Marketing Specialist: Vision and Goals

Flexible Vision for Marketing Specialist

My passion lies in crafting compelling marketing strategies that resonate with diverse audiences. I'll experiment with different channels like social media, content marketing, and email marketing, constantly analyze data to optimize campaigns, and refine my approach. I'm open to exploring various marketing specializations or industries, allowing me to tailor my skills to a niche market and to identify the best fit for my talents. I seek to create impactful marketing solutions that not only meet business objectives but also enhance customer experience.

Flexible Goal 1: Achieve a high level of proficiency in using various channels like social media, content marketing, and email marketing to engage audiences and deliver effective campaigns.

Fixed Goal 2: Acquire practical marketing experience across a variety of industries to understand diverse market dynamics and customer preferences.

Fixed Goal 3: After gaining experience and exploring different aspects of marketing, pinpoint a specific specialization and industry that aligns best with my skills and passion.

- **Figure 2.5:** This figure demonstrates how a vision for becoming a director of digital marketing can be distilled into two specific goals. It provides a graphic depiction of the goals, illustrating how they relate to each other and lead to the vision.

Figure 2.5. Director of Digital Marketing: Vision and Goals

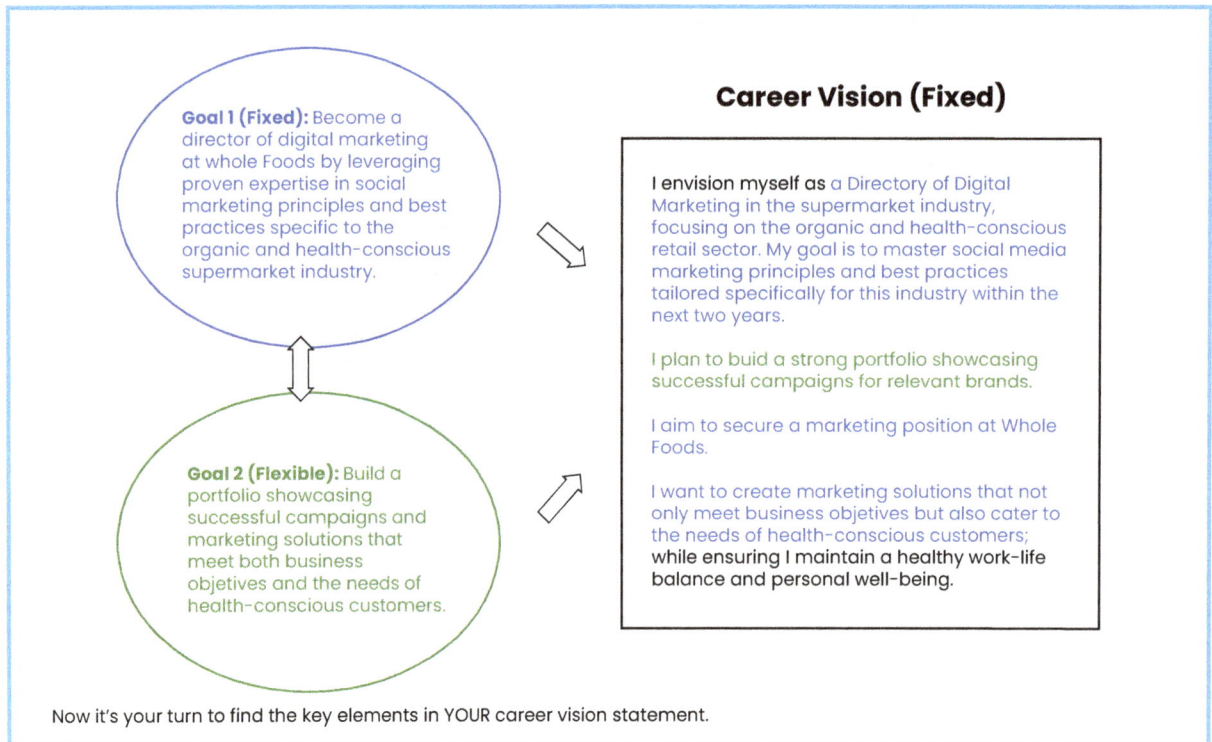

Goal 1 (Fixed): Become a director of digital marketing at whole Foods by leveraging proven expertise in social marketing principles and best practices specific to the organic and health-conscious supermarket industry.

Goal 2 (Flexible): Build a portfolio showcasing successful campaigns and marketing solutions that meet both business objectives and the needs of health-conscious customers.

Career Vision (Fixed)

I envision myself as a Directory of Digital Marketing in the supermarket industry, focusing on the organic and health-conscious retail sector. My goal is to master social media marketing principles and best practices tailored specifically for this industry within the next two years.

I plan to buid a strong portfolio showcasing successful campaigns for relevant brands.

I aim to secure a marketing position at Whole Foods.

I want to create marketing solutions that not only meet business objetives but also cater to the needs of health-conscious customers; while ensuring I maintain a healthy work-life balance and personal well-being.

Now it's your turn to find the key elements in YOUR career vision statement.

INSIGHT EXERCISE 2.7. IDENTIFYING KEY ELEMENTS IN YOUR CAREER VISION

In the first box, write your career vision statement. Using **Figure 2.3** and **Figure 2.4** for reference, underline the key elements in the statement and use the second box to indicate the goals needed to reach your vision. Circle whether the goal is fixed or flexible.

If your career vision involves upskilling or reskilling, refer to the **Enhancing Your AI Skills: Top Training Resources** section at the end of the chapter.

Your Vision	*Your Goals to Reach Your Vision:*
	Fixed or Flexible Goal 1:
	Fixed or Flexible Goal 2:

Now that you have set your goals, it's time to embark on the learning journey inspired by your career vision. The next step in the SEAM model is to ACT, which you will begin in the upcoming section.

LEARNING LOCK-IN

What new thing did you learn about yourself by crafting your career vision statement?

Chapter 2: Resources

ALL ABOUT FEEDBACK

Navigating your career, whether employed, seeking employment, or managing it outside a traditional work setting, requires gathering feedback from others. By establishing a clear process for soliciting and utilizing feedback, you can ensure continuous learning, growth, and alignment of your career development with your professional goals and market demands.

TIMING THE ASK

There are several critical moments in your career journey when seeking feedback can be particularly beneficial. Here are some key situations where a fresh perspective can help you get back on track and continue progressing towards your goals:

- **Experiencing Stress or Doubt About Your Career Path:** At such a challenging time, seeking feedback can provide reassurance and guidance to help you move forward.
- **Feeling Overwhelmed by Life and Needing to Reassess Your Professional Goals:** Life changes or overwhelming responsibilities might necessitate a reassessment of your goals. Feedback can help you balance these aspects and make necessary adjustments.
- **Finding the Preparation for Your Career to Be Too Challenging:** If you're struggling with difficult learning material, training, or instructors, feedback can offer new strategies or resources to make the learning process more manageable and effective.
- **Finding the Required Information Surrounding Your Career to Be Unengaging:** If the material does not connect with you, feedback can help you find ways to make it more interesting or connect it to your larger career goals.
- **Disinterest in Career Development Activities Required to Advance:** If you're disinterested in the activities needed for progression, feedback can help you to find alternative paths or motivate you to stay on track.
- **Having Trouble Completing the Necessary Tasks:** Struggling with task completion can be a sign that you need help refining your approach. Feedback can provide practical tips or adjustments to your plan.

- **Considering Pivoting or Doing Something Completely Different:** Major career shifts can be daunting. Feedback can help you evaluate the pros and cons, ensuring that your decision is well-informed and aligned with your long-term goals.

ASKING FOR FEEDBACK

If you have not asked someone for feedback before, it might feel strange at first, but don't be intimidated. Most people find it a compliment to be asked and will readily help you if their time permits. And, if they cannot help you, they will surely be honest about it. Here are the most used ways to solicit professional feedback:

- **One-on-One Meetings:** Schedule a one-on-one meeting with your manager or mentor to discuss progress and receive feedback on your career goals. These meetings can provide a safe space for open and honest dialogue.
- **360-Degree Feedback:** This method involves gathering feedback from all individuals you interact with at work, including superiors, peers, and subordinates. It yields a well-rounded view of your professional interactions and performance.

- **Feedback Forms:** Use anonymous surveys or feedback forms that colleagues and clients can fill out. This method can help gather candid responses and is particularly useful for collecting feedback from a larger group.
- **Performance Reviews:** Participate in formal performance review sessions that are typically part of an organization's HR process. Ask probing questions about your career vision and record what you hear.
- **Informal Feedback Channels:** Encourage regular, informal feedback during team meetings or casual interactions. This ongoing feedback can be less intimidating and more conducive to continual improvement.

WHAT TO DO WITH THE FEEDBACK

Feedback is meant to be internalized and acted upon.

- **Document Feedback:** Keep a record of all feedback received and analyze it to identify common themes or areas for improvement.
- **Incorporate Feedback in Your Action Plan:** Make sure to update your action plan based on the feedback you receive.

- **Consider Consistency:** Compare the feedback with input you've received from other trusted sources. If multiple sources are highlighting the same areas, it's likely an indicator of its validity and importance.

EXPRESSING GRATITUDE

Make sure that you let the person who is giving you feedback know that you are grateful for their help. Here are some ways to do it:

- **Express Gratitude Directly:** Send a personalized thank-you note or message expressing appreciation for specific feedback, highlighting how their insights have been valuable.
- **Share Your Progress:** Update those who provided feedback on how their suggestions are making a difference in your overall career journey. This keeps them engaged in your progress and shows that their advice has been impactful.
- **Offer Reciprocal Feedback:** If appropriate, offer constructive feedback or support in return, fostering a mutual and beneficial relationship. This not only strengthens professional connections but also shows your willingness to engage in a supportive community.

Feedback is a valuable component of SEAM and continuing to improve upon your career journey. Don't be shy; ask for feedback!

ENHANCING YOUR AI SKILLS: TOP TRAINING RESOURCES

As you navigate your career journey, staying informed and up-to-date with the latest advancements in AI is crucial. The following list includes top AI training resources from industry leaders like IBM, Amazon, Microsoft, and Google. These platforms offer a range of courses and certifications that cater to different skill levels and professional needs. Dive into these resources to enhance your AI expertise and keep your skills future-proof. (Note: The availability and specifics of these resources may evolve over time.)

1. **IBM**
- **IBM AI Engineering Professional Certificate:** Learn AI engineering skills, including deep learning, machine learning, and neural networks, using tools like Python and PyTorch. Available on popular online learning platforms.
- **IBM SkillsBuild:** Access free foundational courses in AI, including an introduction to generative AI fundamentals.

2. **Amazon Web Services (AWS)**
- **AWS Training and Certification:** Offers a wide range of courses on AI and machine learning, from foundational to advanced levels.
- **Generative AI Courses:** AWS provides free courses for business leaders and technologists covering generative AI fundamentals.

3. **Microsoft**
- **Microsoft Learn:** A comprehensive set of AI courses and certifications, including Azure AI Fundamentals and other advanced topics.
- **Virtual Training Days:** One-day digital events that cover AI fundamentals, generative AI, and Microsoft Copilot.

4. **Google**
- **Google AI Training:** Provides educational resources, including courses and tutorials on machine learning and AI concepts, available through the Google AI platform.

By tapping into these resources, you can stay ahead in the fast-evolving AI landscape and ensure your skills remain relevant and in demand.

Chapter 3

ACT:
From Planning to Execution

"Intention is the compass, action the course. We navigate the seas of possibility, charting our own destiny."
Madeleine F. Wallace, Ph.D.

The Act step is where your career plan comes to life. You will develop and execute a comprehensive career action plan based on your work in the Envision step.

Figure 3.1 (see next page) illustrates the key components:

- **Career Vision:** What you aspire to achieve through intentional work.
- **Goals:** Actions that will help you achieve your career vision.
- **Sprint Outcomes:** The results you expect to achieve by completing a set of tasks. These results move you closer to achieving your goals.
- **Tasks:** The activities you need to complete to accomplish each sprint outcome.
- **Key Performance Indicators (KPIs):** Measurable values that determine if your efforts are leading you toward your goals, allowing you to adjust your activities as needed.

Having a written plan is imperative to achieving your career vision. If it's not written, it won't happen. Relying on memory to recall details and decisions is risky and often leads to missed opportunities.

A WRITTEN PLAN . . .

- ✓ Provides a clear and structured roadmap for your career aspirations.
- ✓ Serves as a motivational tool to stay focused and resilient during challenging times.
- ✓ Helps you adapt as new opportunities arise and circumstances change.
- ✓ Offers a reflective perspective on your actions, boosting your confidence and morale.
- ✓ Allows you to track progress effectively, ensuring you are moving toward your goals.

Your Act step will have three parts:
PART I: Visualizing Your Career Journey
PART II: Building Blocks for Your Career Action Plan
PART III: Putting the Building Blocks in Action

Figure 3.1. Components of the Career Action Plan in the SEAM Framework

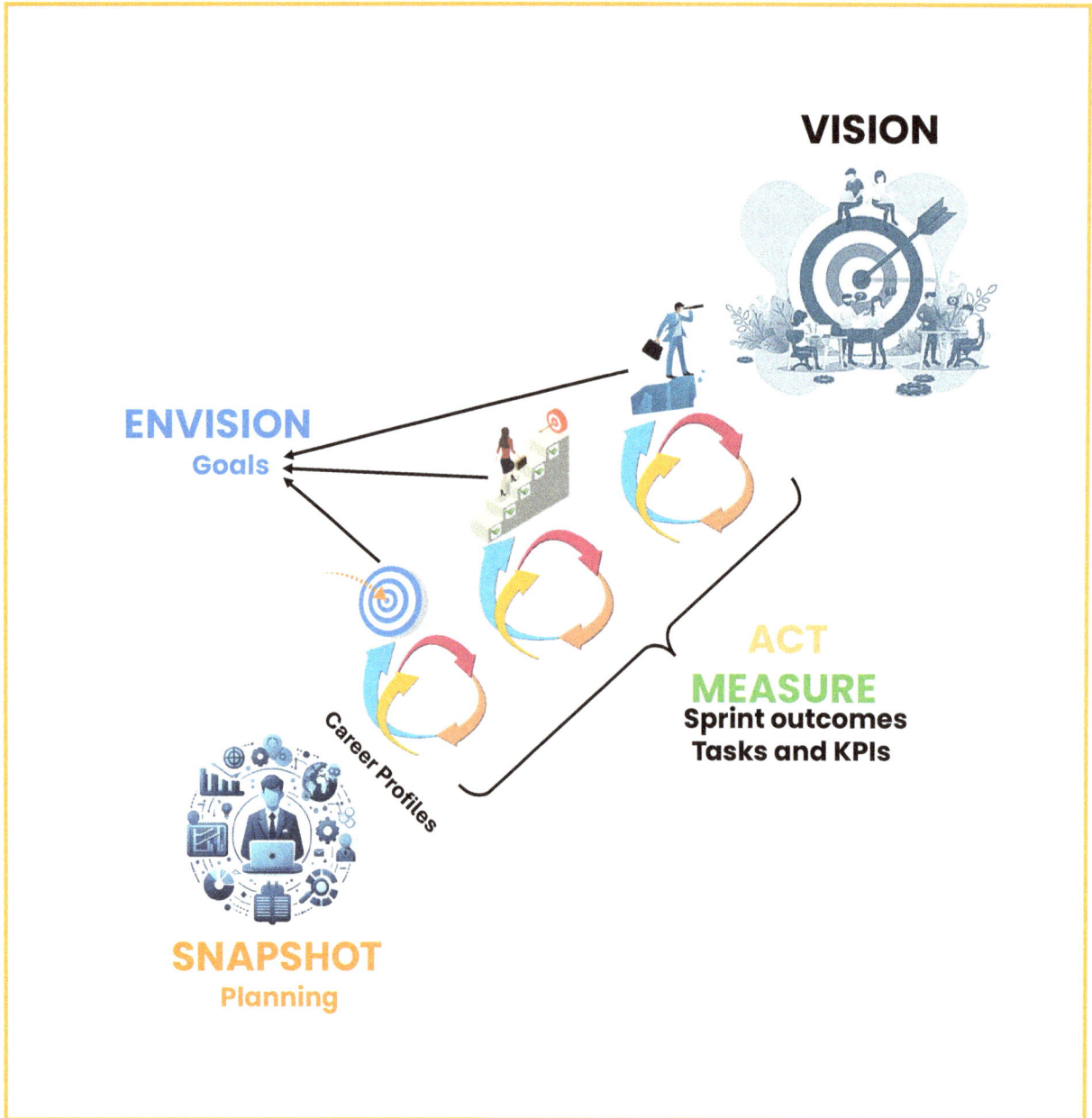

VISION

ENVISION
Goals

Career Profiles

ACT
MEASURE
Sprint outcomes
Tasks and KPIs

SNAPSHOT
Planning

IS A SOFTWARE TOOL NECESSARY?

Everyone has their own preferences and comfort levels when it comes to using software tools. While creating an action plan by hand is possible, the many connected pieces—vision, goals, sprint outcomes, tasks, KPIs—often lead people to use software tools. These tools help with organization, planning, executing the plan, and measuring progress. However, I always recommend outlining the plan on paper first to ensure no details are overlooked before programming it into the software.

INFO SNIPPET
Considerations for Selecting Software Tools

There are three major areas to consider when looking for a software tool:

- **Platform Accessibility:** Ensure the tool allows access from multiple devices, including mobile phones, tablets, and desktops. Cloud-based storage options enhance convenience, enabling you to work on your goals and update your progress from anywhere, at any time.
- **Integration with Other Tools:** Choose a tool that integrates well with applications you frequently use, like email, calendar, and communication platforms, to streamline your career plan.
- **Feature Set:** Look for tools with customizable features for setting milestones, tracking progress, and adjusting plans. If you're a visual person, opt for tools that offer graphs, charts, and other visual representations to help you understand your progress more clearly.

For more information about software tools, see **Which Software Tool is Right for You?** in Resources at the end of the chapter.

ACT PART I: VISUALIZING YOUR CAREER JOURNEY

CREATING A COMPELLING VISUAL ROADMAP

Creating a graphical representation of your career action plan, like a flowchart or interconnected boxes, is essential. It helps you visualize your goals, the sequence of sprints to achieve them, and your career vision. This roadmap keeps you focused on the big picture, even when your attention wanders.

The power of these visuals goes beyond a static plan. Many software tools allow you to track your progress in real-time, providing valuable insights into your journey. This functionality lets you see how far you've come and what's next. You can then choose to display your progress on your computer screen, mobile device, or even print a physical copy for reference.

Figure 3.1 illustrates a visual roadmap for a career action plan. Goals are essential to achieve a career vision and sprints are necessary to accomplish these goals. Each sprint consists of tasks, and each task has key performance indicators (KPIs) that track your progress towards task completion, it is the collective success of all components that make achieving a career goal possible.

INFO SNIPPET
Inspiration vs. Strategy

While both tools can be valuable, it's essential to understand the differences between a visual roadmap and a vision board:

Visual Roadmap:
- A strategic tool outlining the steps to achieve your goals.
- Provides a clear and structured pathway.
- Breaks down your career vision into actionable goals, sprints, tasks, and key performance indicators (KPIs).
- Guides your actions and allows you to track your progress.

Vision Board:
- A collection of images and affirmations.
- Represents your dreams and aspirations.
- Primarily serves to inspire and motivate you.

Figure 3.2. Visual Roadmap of a Career Action Plan

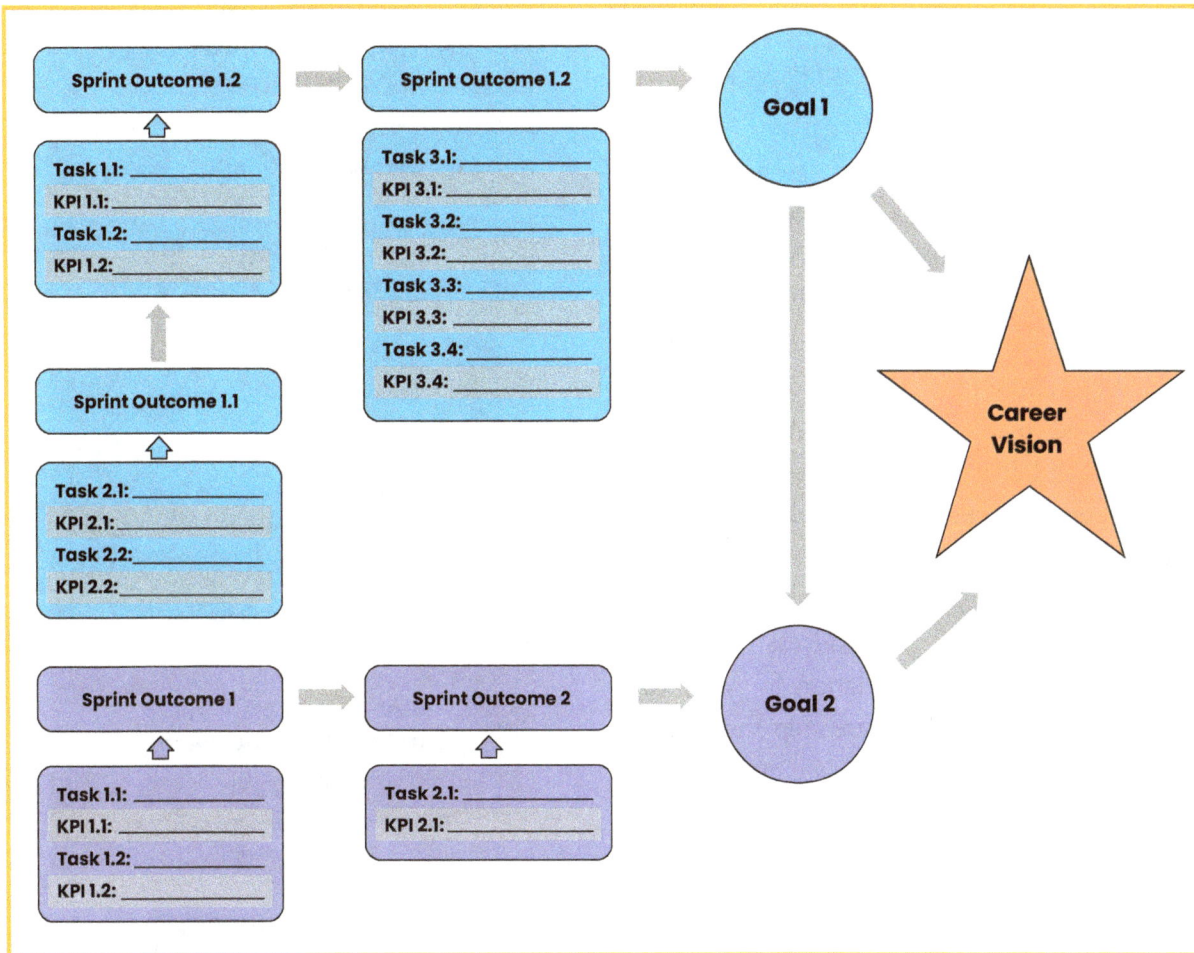

Whether you choose to write everything down in this workbook, use a software tool, or create a table in Excel, the key is to maintain a clear and organized record of your journey. The method you use is less important than ensuring you consistently track your progress and make necessary adjustments to stay on course toward achieving your career goals.

ACT PART II:
BUILDING BLOCKS FOR
YOUR CAREER ACTION PLAN

In SEAM, there are eight essential building blocks for developing and implementing your career action plan. This structured approach empowers you to clearly define your career goals, break them down into manageable components (sprints), and outline specific tasks needed to achieve each sprint outcome. It incorporates KPIs to measure progress, along with assessment methods and reflection to ensure continuous improvement.

In the Act step, we address Blocks 1 through 6, laying the foundation for your career action plan. The Measure step then shifts focus to Blocks 7 and 8, where we evaluate our results and make necessary adjustments. Now, let's dive into the six building blocks that are essential for developing and implementing your career action plan.

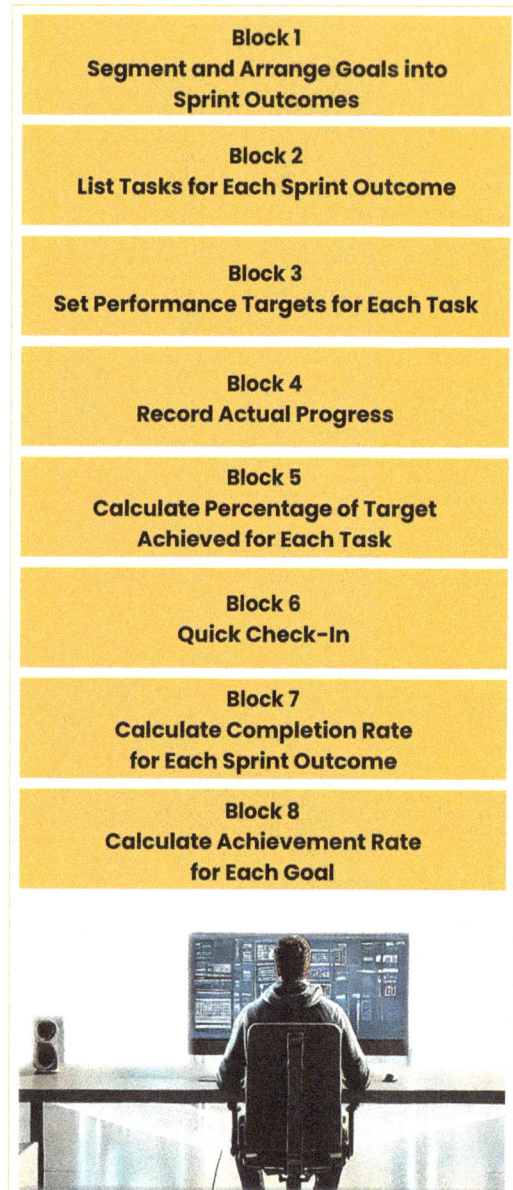

Block 1
Segment and Arrange Goals into Sprint Outcomes

Block 2
List Tasks for Each Sprint Outcome

Block 3
Set Performance Targets for Each Task

Block 4
Record Actual Progress

Block 5
Calculate Percentage of Target Achieved for Each Task

Block 6
Quick Check-In

Block 7
Calculate Completion Rate for Each Sprint Outcome

Block 8
Calculate Achievement Rate for Each Goal

✓ Block 1: Segment and Arrange Goals into Sprint Outcomes

To effectively achieve career goals, start by breaking each goal into smaller, manageable components, each represented as a sprint. Clearly define the desired outcome for each sprint and arrange these sprints in a logical sequence. Some sprints will naturally follow one another, while others may require strategic planning to decide whether to approach them sequentially or concurrently.

Director of Digital Marketing Example

Figure 3.3 illustrates this process using two examples: Goal 1 (fixed) and Goal 2 (flexible) from the director of digital marketing scenario outlined in the Envision step.

- **Goal 1 (Fixed):** This goal follows a structured progression where each sprint builds toward a leadership role in digital marketing. It starts with acquiring relevant knowledge and skills (Sprint Outcome 1.1), progresses to enhancing leadership and project management abilities (Sprint Outcome 1.2), and culminates in taking actionable steps, such as submitting job applications (Sprint Outcome 1.3).

- **Goal 2 (Flexible):** This goal focuses on developing tangible outputs that enhance career prospects. It begins with the practical application of generative AI skills learned in Goal 1, applying them to real-world projects (Sprint Outcome 2.1). The next step is to develop case studies showcasing successful marketing campaigns (Sprint Outcome 2.2), which are then used to build a professional portfolio. This portfolio not only contributes to achieving Goal 2 but also strengthens job applications by providing concrete evidence of expertise and success.

By combining the structured acquisition of essential skills with their practical application, this dual-goal approach offers a comprehensive pathway for advancement in digital marketing. It ensures that individuals gain both the necessary expertise and demonstrate their abilities through tangible results. This methodical strategy is highly effective for aspiring directors of digital marketing, as it provides them with the knowledge and proven track record needed for leadership success.

Figure 3.3. Pathway to a Digital Marketing Leadership Role: Fixed and Flexible Goals

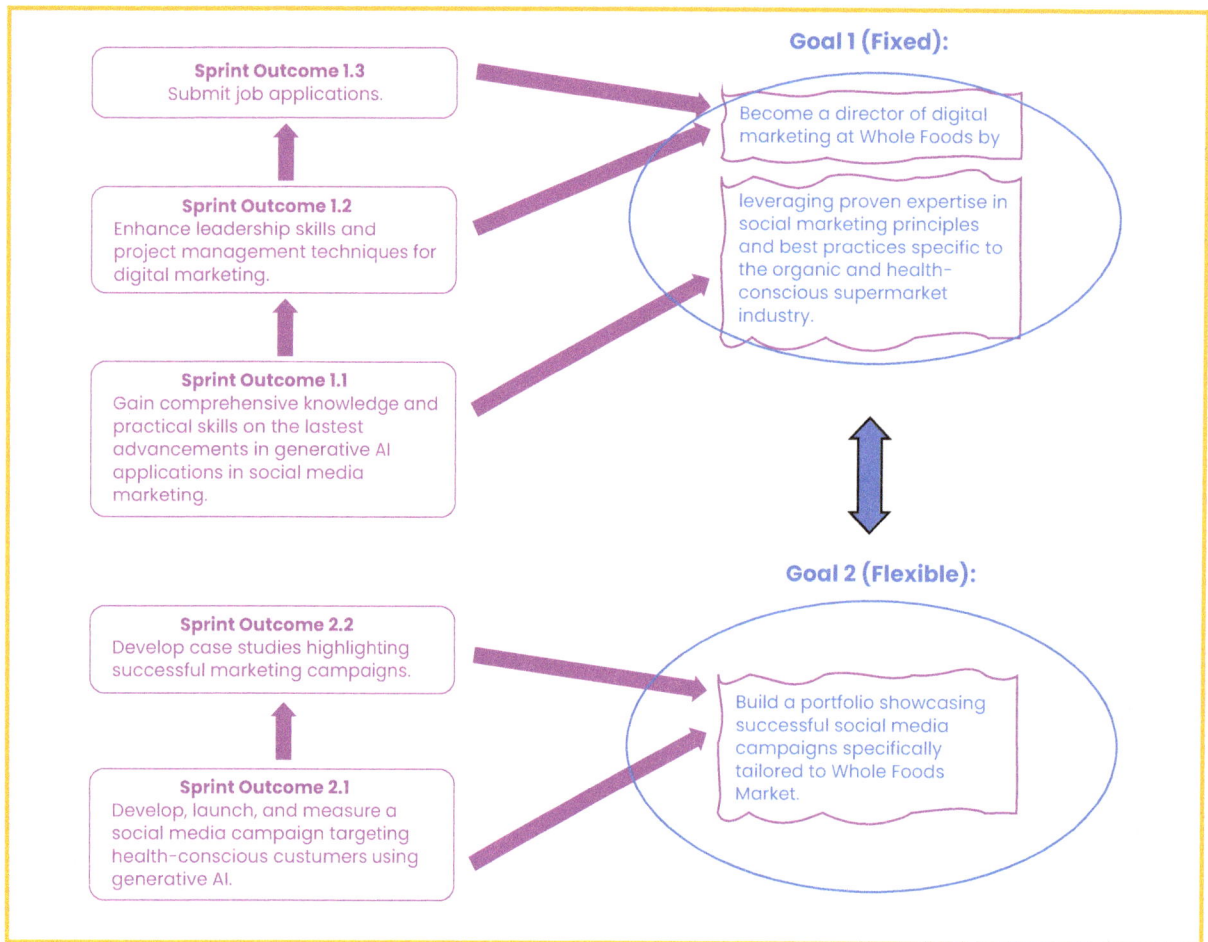

Goal 1 (Fixed):

Become a director of digital marketing at Whole Foods by

leveraging proven expertise in social marketing principles and best practices specific to the organic and health-conscious supermarket industry.

Sprint Outcome 1.3
Submit job applications.

Sprint Outcome 1.2
Enhance leadership skills and project management techniques for digital marketing.

Sprint Outcome 1.1
Gain comprehensive knowledge and practical skills on the lastest advancements in generative AI applications in social media marketing.

Goal 2 (Flexible):

Build a portfolio showcasing successful social media campaigns specifically tailored to Whole Foods Market.

Sprint Outcome 2.2
Develop case studies highlighting successful marketing campaigns.

Sprint Outcome 2.1
Develop, launch, and measure a social media campaign targeting health-conscious custumers using generative AI.

✓ **Block 2: List Tasks for Each Sprint Outcome**

Identify the specific tasks needed for each sprint outcome, detailing the steps to complete each one.

✓ **Block 3: Set Performance Targets for Each Task**

Set specific, measurable performance targets to guide your progress toward each task. These targets will later serve as reference points for assessing your achievements (Wallace, 2023). When setting targets, consider the following:

- **Baseline:** Establish a current baseline to measure improvement over time. For example, if you attended five webinars last year, that number serves as your baseline.
- **Target:** Define a clear, achievable target for improvement. For instance, to increase engagement, aim to attend ten webinars this year, effectively doubling last year's attendance for a 100% increase. Specify a timeframe, such as January to December, for this target.
- **Metric:** Ensure that the targets are quantifiable with measurable values like numbers, percentages, or binary outcomes (e.g., yes/no). In the webinar example, the metric could be the number of webinars attended, with a goal of ten for the year.

✓ **Block 4: Record Actual Progress**

Document the results of each task as you complete it. Maintaining accurate records will help you monitor progress and make adjustments as needed.

✓ **Block 5: Calculate Percentage of Target Achieved for Each Task**

To assess KPI achievement, divide the actual value by the target value and multiply by 100. For yes/no indicators, a "yes" result equals 100% achieved.

✓ **Block 6: Quick Check-In**

After completing a task, note any challenges faced and how they were overcome

Figure 3.4 illustrates the blocks technique as applied to the Director of Digital Marketing career action plan example. Blocks 7 and 8 will be introduced in the Measure step in the next chapter.

Figure 3.4. Blocks Technique Applied to the Director of Digital Marketing Career Action Plan

Goal 1: Become a director of digital marketing at Whole Foods by leveraging proven expertise in social marketing principles and best practices specific to the organic and health-conscious supermarket industry.

Block 1	Block 6	Block 2	Block 3	Block 4	Block 5

Sprint Outcome	Task	Target	Actual Value	% of Target Achieved
Sprint Outcome 1.1: Gain comprehensive knowledge and practical skills on the latest advancements in generative AI applications in social media marketing. **Start Date:** MM/DD/YY *(Task 1.1.1 start date)* **End Date:** MM/DD/YY *(Task 1.1.2 end date)*	**Task 1.1.1 Start Date:** MM/DD/YY **End Date:** MM/DD/YY Obtain a generative AI Large Language Models (LLMs) certification. **Baseline:** Beginner level. **Quick Check-in - Challenge:** Grasping the advanced concepts and technical details. **Quick Check-in - Solution:** Enrolled in supplementary online courses and joined study groups.	Obtain one certification within the next three months.	Certification status (1) completed or (0) not completed	$\frac{Actual}{Target}$ x 100
	Task 1.1.2 Start Date: MM/DD/YY **End Date:** MM/DD/YY Complete a practical project using generative AI in social media marketing **Baseline:** No previous practical project experience in generative AI applications. **Quick Check-in - Challenge:** Integrating generative AI tools into the existing marketing strategy. **Quick Check-in - Solution:** Sought guidance from online communities to troubleshoot integration.	Complete the project within two months after certification	Project Completion (1) completed or (0) not completed	$\frac{Actual}{Target}$ x 100
Completion Rate Sprint Outcome 1.1	**Total**			

Block 7

Figure 3.4. Blocks Technique Applied to the Director of Digital Marketing Career Action Plan (continued)

Sprint Outcome	Task	Target	Actual Value	% of Target Achieved
Sprint Outcome 1.2: Enhance leadership skills and project management techniques for digital marketing. **Start Date:** MM/DD/YY *(Task 1.2.1 start date)* **End Date:** MM/DD/YY *(Task 1.2.1 end date)*	**Task 1.2.1** **Start Date:** MM/DD/YY **End Date:** MM/DD/YY Participate in a leadership webinar series tailored for digital marketing managers. **Baseline:** Participated in one manager training one year ago. **Quick Check-in - Challenge:** Aligning webinar timings with work and personal commitments. **Quick Check-in - Solution:** Communicated with team members to ensure minimal work conflicts.	Participate in five leadership webinars within the next two months.	Number of webinars attended: 4	$\frac{Actual}{Target}$ x 100
Sprint Outcome 1.3: Submit job applications. **Start Date:** MM/DD/YY *(Task 1.3.1 start date)* **End Date:** MM/DD/YY *(Task 1.3.1 end date)*	**Task 1.3.1** **Start Date:** MM/DD/YY **End Date:** MM/DD/YY Submit job applications. **Baseline:** No job applications submitted. **Quick Check-in - Challenge:** Time-consuming to tailor each job application. **Quick Check-in - Solution:** Created templates for resumes and cover letters.	Submit applications to at least six job openings within the next six months.	Number of job applications submitted: 2	$\frac{Actual}{Target}$ x 100
Completion Rate Sprint Outcome 1.1	**Total**			
Goal 1 Achievement Rate	**Grand Total**			

Block 8

REFLECT AND PREPARE FOR YOUR CAREER ACTION PLAN

As you prepare to create your action plan in the next section, using a template similar to the one we used for the Director of Digital Marketing example, take another look at **Figures 3.3** and **3.4** to see how concepts from Blocks 1 through 6 are applied in the career action plan.

Remember, as I mentioned at the beginning of this chapter, I recommend starting on paper—now is the perfect time for you to do the same. Begin by jotting down sprint outcomes aligned with your goals, detailing the tasks needed to achieve those outcomes, and defining KPIs to measure your progress. Reflect on what feels clear and where you might need additional clarity. You're almost there—trust the process and take it one step at a time!

IDEA GEM
Anchored In Focus

When I dive into a project that demands deep focus, I begin with a grounding ritual. I set up my workspace by a window, soaking in natural light, and carefully arrange everything I might need within reach—water, snacks, music, a picture of the ocean, and a bit of chewing gum—each item a quiet commitment to staying fully present. I start by immersing myself in reading something relevant to the topic I'm working on, letting curiosity ignite ideas that build like waves. When my mind wanders, I find calm in a picture of my childhood beach—a place of simplicity and resilience. The ocean has always been my anchor, steadying me as I navigate the vast sea of work and ideas..

ACT PART III: PUTTING THE BUILDING BLOCKS IN ACTION

Now, it's your turn to put what you've learned into practice by creating a career plan of action using the building blocks.

Based on both research and my own experience, focusing on one or two goals at a time significantly increases the likelihood of success. Studies have shown that when individuals spread their efforts across multiple objectives, their commitment and effectiveness tend to dilute, making it harder to achieve success in any of the goals (Clear, 2018). I have seen this principle hold true in my own work and when working with my mentees, where concentrated effort on a limited number of goals has consistently led to more impactful and sustainable results. However, this focus on fewer goals is particularly crucial at the beginning. As you gain more experience, you can gradually add a couple more goals without compromising your effectiveness.

To implement this approach:

- **Work on one goal at a time** (certainly no more than two).
- **Outline no more than three or four sprints per goal.** This helps to keep your efforts manageable and ensures steady progress.
- **Outline no more than three tasks to complete a sprint.** If you find you need more than four tasks to complete a sprint, it indicates that you might need to break it down into additional sprints to effectively reach your goal.

SCIENCE SPOTLIGHT
Process Visualization for Goal Achievement

Research shows that process visualization, which involves imagining the steps needed to achieve a goal, is significantly more effective than outcome visualization, which focuses on the end result. Students participating in the study who visualized their actions—such as organizing study sessions and minimizing distractions—were better prepared, stayed motivated, and achieved their academic goals more effectively. Focus on visualizing the journey, not just the destination, for greater success (Alghazo et al., 2020).

INSIGHT EXERCISE 3.1.
MY CAREER ACTION PLAN

Now it's time to turn your draft ideas from the previous section into an actionable plan. Use the template on the next page to officially map out your work plan with the building blocks approach. Take your time—every career journey is unique, and there's no need to aim for perfection. Click the QR code to download Fillable PDFs featuring the building blocks approach and built-in formulas to simplify calculations, helping you stay focused on your goals.

If you're using planning software or a mobile app, take a moment to understand how to enter your goals and track progress. Compare the tool's features with the building blocks approach in the Fillable PDFs to see which best supports your plan. Many find the PDF format particularly convenient for its ready-to-use structure, but ultimately, the choice is yours. Why? Mastering the art of creating a structured action plan is a valuable management skill—the same principles apply when developing business plans, preparing you for greater leadership and strategic thinking. The tool calculates progress and outcomes.

Access Fillable PDFs for Insight Exercises at madeleinewallace.com/resources-ai

INSIGHT EXERCISE 3.1.
MY CAREER ACTION PLAN

Goal 1:				
Sprint Outcome	**Task**	**Target**	**Actual Value**	**% of Target Achieved**
Sprint Outcome 1.1:	**Task 1.1.1** **Start** **Date:** MM/DD/YY **End Date:** MM/DD/YY Baseline:			
	Quick Check-in - Challenge: Quick Check-in - Solution:			
	Task 1.1.2 **Start** **Date:** MM/DD/YY **End Date:** MM/DD/YY Baseline:			
	Quick Check-in - Challenge: Quick Check-in - Solution:			
	Task 1.1.3 **Start** **Date:** MM/DD/YY **End Date:** MM/DD/YY Baseline:			
Start Date: MM/DD/YY *(Task 1.1.1 start date)* **End Date:** MM/DD/YY *(Task 1.1.3 end date)*	Quick Check-in - Challenge: Quick Check-in - Solution:			
Completion Rate Sprint Outcome 1.1	**Total**			

Sprint Outcome	Task	Target	Actual Value	% of Target Achieved
Sprint Outcome 1.2:	Task 1.2.1 **Start Date:** MM/DD/YY **End Date:** MM/DD/YY **Baseline:**			
	Quick Check-in - Challenge: **Quick Check-in - Solution:**			
	Task 1.2.2 **Start Date:** MM/DD/YY **End Date:** MM/DD/YY **Baseline:**			
	Quick Check-in - Challenge: **Quick Check-in - Solution:**			
	Task 1.2.3 **Start Date:** MM/DD/YY **End Date:** MM/DD/YY **Baseline:**			
Start Date: MM/DD/YY *(Task 1.2.1 start date)* **End Date:** MM/DD/YY *(Task 1.2.3 end date)*	**Quick Check-in - Challenge:** **Quick Check-in - Solution:**			
Completion Rate Sprint Outcome 1.2	**Total**			

Congratulations! You have now set up what you need to work towards your career development and determined how you will do it.

Next, we will move on to the final step of the process—Measure.

LEARNING LOCK-IN

What can you do for yourself to stay personally motivated through your sprints?

Chapter 3: Resources

WHICH SOFTWARE TOOL IS RIGHT FOR YOU?

Tools like Trello and Asana are ideal for managing career development and personal projects. They enable you to set specific milestones, track skill development, and conduct regular performance reviews to effectively assess and adjust your progress towards career goals effectively. More importantly, they facilitate easy updating and revising of goals, embodying SEAM's career framework.

TRELLO'S MAIN FEATURES

https://trello.com/

Trello is a tool used for visual collaboration tool that helps teams organize projects into boards to plan, manage, and celebrate their work. It's based on the Kanban system, a popular methodology for lean management. Trello can be used for any project, workflow, or team type, including marketing, product management, engineering, and design.

- **Boards, Lists, and Cards:** Organize projects into boards, which contain lists (stages of the project) and cards (individual tasks). This visual arrangement helps track progress.

- **Custom Labels and Tags:** Customize cards with labels for quick identification of task types or priority levels.
- **Automation:** Utilize Butler, Trello's built-in automation tool, to automate repetitive actions like moving cards, sending reminders, or updating task statuses.
- **Integrations (Power-Ups):** Enhance functionality with integrations like Google Drive for attaching documents or Calendar for due dates that sync with your personal calendar.

ASANA MAIN FEATURES

https://asana.com/

Asana provides various views (like lists, boards, calendars, and timelines) to accommodate different project management styles. It also integrates with other tools, such as Slack, Google Drive, and Zoom, to streamline workflows. Asana is used by teams across industries to improve collaboration, increase transparency, and ensure that projects are completed efficiently. Operationalize goals Connect work to company goals Automate workflows across departments.

connects work across different departments. Connect work to goals and automate workflows with AI as your teammate.

- **Task Dependencies:** Set up dependencies between tasks to ensure they are completed in the correct order, which is ideal for projects with multiple moving parts.
- **Timeline View:** Visualize your project timeline and adjust schedules as needed by dragging and dropping tasks on the timeline.
- **Workload Management:** Use the Workload feature to see how much work each team member has at any time, helping balance loads and prevent burnout.
- **Custom Fields:** Add custom fields to tasks to track specific data points relevant to your goals, like time spent, cost, or project status.

GOAL-SETTING APPS
(e.g., https://goalsontrack.com/, https://lifetick.com/)

Goal-setting apps are specifically designed for personal goal management, focusing more on individual progress and less on team collaboration.

- **Progress Tracking:** Visualize your progress with charts and graphs, making it easy to see how close you are to achieving your goals.
- **Habit Tracking:** Some apps include features to help you build habits that align with your goals, providing reminders and consistency checks.
- **Journaling and Reflection:** Maintain a journal or diary within the app to reflect on your progress, challenges, and learnings, which is essential for long-term goal adjustment and personal growth.

COMPARISON OF KPIS AND SMART GOALS

Why I Prefer KPIs Over SMART Goals: As an entrepreneur, I find KPIs to be a more effective tool for career development and business growth. Unlike SMART goals, which are specific, measurable, achievable, relevant, and time-bound, KPIs offer a more dynamic and adaptable approach. They provide continuous metrics that allow for real-time monitoring, immediate feedback, and quick adjustments—crucial elements in career development.

KPIs enable a holistic view by encompassing both quantitative and qualitative indicators, ensuring comprehensive assessment of progress. Their adaptability to changing goals or industry landscapes makes KPIs an ideal choice for guiding and achieving long-term career success.

Aspect	KPIs (Key Performance Indicators)	SMART Goals (Specific, Measurable, Achievable, Relevant, Time-bound)
Monitoring and Feedback	Provide continuous metrics for real-time progress monitoring, allowing for immediate feedback and quick adjustments.	Outline targets within a timeframe, but lack a mechanism for continuous monitoring, relying on end-point reviews.
Measurements	Encompass both quantitative and qualitative indicators, allowing assessment of diverse aspects of career progress.	Typically focused on specific outcomes, potentially overlooking important qualitative elements.
Adaptability and Flexibility	Are highly adaptable and can adjust benchmarks as career goals or industry landscapes change, offering flexibility.	Adaptable, but often requires significant reassessment and restructuring of the goal itself.
Application Across Goals	Can be relevant to multiple goals simultaneously, e.g., a KPI on networking efforts can advance several career objectives like gaining promotions or industry knowledge	Usually isolated with specific metrics, which may lead to a compartmentalized approach in career planning.
Motivation and Engagement	Provide continuous motivation and help maintain momentum by achieving small wins as evidenced with the ongoing tracking and visibility of incremental improvements.	Effective in setting precise targets, but motivation may decrease over long periods without intermediate milestones or reassessments.

Chapter 4

MEASURE:
Tracking Your Achievement

"Lost at sea without a wind rose?
Track your efforts and navigate to
your goals."

Madeleine F. Wallace, Ph.D.

The Measure step is designed to provide you with a structured approach to assess the progress made in the Act step, reflect on your performance, and set new directions as you continue your career journey.

Remember that measuring your progress is not just about tallying successes and identifying areas for improvement. It's about celebrating how far you've come, learning from your experiences, and refining your approach to continue growing.

Your career development is an ongoing journey. Every sprint outcome you reach and lesson you learn contributes to your overall growth. By regularly assessing your progress, you ensure that you remain adaptable and prepared for the opportunities and challenges ahead.

In this step, we will focus on three key parts:
PART I: Monitoring Your Achievements
PART II: Establishing Benchmarks and Interpreting Results
PART III: Cultivating a Career of Continuous Growth

Let's dive in and start measuring your journey to success. Embrace the process of evaluation and reflection—it's a powerful tool that will keep you aligned with your goals and motivated to achieve your career vision.

SCIENCE SPOTLIGHT
Seeing Progress Fuels Your Drive

Research has shown that monitoring your progress is crucial for achieving your goals. Harkin et al. (2016) examined 138 studies and found that interventions designed to promote progress monitoring significantly increased both the frequency of monitoring and goal attainment. Here are the findings:

- Participants who engaged in progress monitoring were more likely to track their progress consistently.
- Those who monitored their progress were also more successful in achieving their goals.
- The positive effects of monitoring were amplified when progress was reported publicly or physically recorded.

Practical Tips:
- **Public Accountability:** Share your progress with a trusted peer, coach, or mentor.
- **Track Your Wins**: Keep a journal or app to document your achievements and setbacks.

MEASURE PART I: MONITORING YOUR ACHIEVEMENTS

In SEAM, progress is monitored using KPIs at key milestones: after the completion of each task (Block 5), each sprint outcome (Block 7), and each goal (Block 8). These critical junctures allow you to make necessary adjustments to your action plan, ensuring your career development stays aligned with your personal aspirations and remains responsive to changes in the professional environment and your experiences.

In the Act step, we covered building Blocks 1 through 6 for developing and implementing your career action plan. Now, in the Measure step, we turn our focus to the remaining building blocks, which help assess progress and guide strategic adjustments.

✓ Block 7: Calculate Completion Rate for Each Sprint Outcome

The completion rate measures the success of each sprint by identifying tasks that were not fully completed, determining if you are on track, and guiding adjustments to tasks that need more focus or refinement.

✓ Block 8: Calculate Achievement Rate for Each Goal

The achievement rate measures the overall success of the entire goal, assessing how well the goal was met. It highlights overarching areas that may need more attention and provides insights into the cumulative impact of all sprints and tasks. This helps determine whether your strategy is effective or if adjustments are needed to align more closely with your overall career vision.

Figure 4.1 provides a quick reference for calculating rates for individual sprints and overall goals in the SEAM framework.

Figure 4.1. Steps for Calculating Completion and Achievement Rates in SEAM

Step	Block 7: Calculate Completion Rate for Each Sprint Outcome	Block 8: Calculate Achievement Rate for Each Goal
1. Identify Targets and Actuals	Identify the target values and actual values achieved for each task within the sprint outcome.	For each sprint outcome related to the goal, gather the total target values and actual values achieved, using the data calculated in Block 7.
2. Sum Targets and Actuals	Sum the target values and actual values for all tasks within the sprint outcome.	Sum the total target values and actual values across all individual sprint outcomes within the goal.
3. Calculate Rate	Use the formula: $$\text{Completion Rate:} \frac{Total\ Actuals}{Total\ Targets} \times 100$$	Use the formula: $$\text{Achievement Rate:} \frac{Total\ Actuals}{Total\ Targets} \times 100$$

Director of Digital Marketing Example

SEAM offers flexibility in crafting your career plan and calculating completion and achievement rates. You can use "My Career Action Plan"—the Fillable PDF from **Insight Exercise 3.1** or any software or app of your choice. The key is understanding how to track progress and ensuring clarity in your tracking and calculation methods.

In Act 3, I used the director of digital marketing example to illustrate a career action plan by applying Blocks 1 through 6 with the Fillable PDF. **Figure 4.2** continues with this example, now incorporating Blocks 7 and 8 to for Goal 1.

- **Calculating Completion Rates (Block 7):** Completion rates for each sprint outcome are calculated by comparing total actuals to total targets. For example, Sprint Outcome 1.1 achieved a 100% completion rate by meeting all its targets, while Sprint Outcome 1.3 had a 33% completion rate as fewer job applications were submitted than targeted.
- **Calculating Achievement Rate (Block 8):** The achievement rate for the overall goal is determined by summing the targets and actuals from all sprint outcomes and calculating a percentage. In this example, the achievement rate for Goal 1 is 62%, indicating the overall progress towards becoming a director of digital marketing.

Figure 4.2. Application of Blocks 7 & 8 in the Director of Digital Marketing Career Plan (Goal 1)

Goal 1: Become a director of digital marketing at Whole Foods by leveraging proven expertise in social marketing principles and best practices specific to the organic and health-conscious supermarket industry.

Sprint Outcome	Task	Target	Actual Value	% of Target Achieved
Sprint Outcome 1.1: Gain comprehensive knowledge and practical skills on the latest advancements in generative AI applications in social media marketing.	**Task 1.1.1** Obtain a generative AI Large Language Models (LLMs) certification	1	1	100%
	Task 1.1.2 Complete a practical project using generative AI in social media marketing	1	1	100%
Completion Rate Sprint Outcome 1.1 ◄ Block 7 **Total**		**1+1=2**	**1+1=2**	**100%** $\frac{\text{Total Actuals}}{\text{Total Targets}} = \frac{2}{2} \times 100$
Sprint Outcome 1.2: Enhance leadership skills and project management techniques for digital marketing.	**Task 1.2.1** Participate in a leadership webinar series tailored for digital marketing managers.	5	4	80%
Completion Rate Sprint Outcome 1.2 **Total**		5	4	80%
Sprint Outcome 1.3: Submit job applications.	**Task 1.3.1** Submit job applications.	6	2	33%
Completion Rate Sprint Outcome 1.3 **Total**		**6**	**2**	**33%**
Goal 1 Achievement Rate **Grand Total**		**2+5+6=13**	**2+4+2=8**	**62%** $\frac{\text{Total Actuals}}{\text{Total Targets}} = \frac{8}{13} \times 100$

Block 8

Figure 4.3 demonstrates the calculation of completion rates and achievement rates for Goal 2, which is centered on building a portfolio of successful campaigns for health-conscious customers. Take a few minutes to study the figure and understand the process of tracking progress. Notice how each sprint outcome is broken down into specific tasks, with target and actual values, and how the completion rates for each sprint are calculated. This figure also shows how these completion rates contribute to the overall achievement rate of the goal. By analyzing this example, you can gain a deeper understanding of how to apply these methods to your own career development goals and measure your success effectively.

Figure 4.3. Application of Blocks 7 & 8 in the Director of Digital Marketing Career Plan (Goal 2)

Goal 2: Build a portfolio showcasing successful campaigns and marketing solutions that meet both business objectives and the needs of health-conscious customers.

Sprint Outcome	Task	Target	Actual Value	% of Target Achieved
Sprint Outcome 2.1: Develop, launch, and measure a social media campaign targeting health-conscious customers using generative AI.	**Task 2.1.1** Identify key trends and preferences among health-conscious customers using research tools and generative AI.	10	8	80%
	Task 2.1.2 Create engaging content leveraging insights from market research and generative AI.	15	12	80%
	Task 2.1.3 Launch the campaign, track, and analyze key engagement metrics (likes, shares, comments) to measure effectiveness	10	9	90%
Completion Rate Sprint Outcome 2.1	**Total**	35	29	83%
Sprint Outcome 2.2: Develop case studies highlighting successful marketing campaigns	**Task 2.2.1** Collect testimonials from previous campaigns.	3	2	67%
	Task 2.2.2 Publish the case studies on the company website and social media.	3	2	67%
Completion Rate Sprint Outcome 2.2	**Total**	6	4	67%
Goal 2 Achievement Rate	**Grand Total**	41	33	80%

Block 7

Block 8

INFO SNIPPET
Mastering Completion and Achievement Rates

In your career journey, understanding how to measure progress is vital for reaching your goals. In the Measure step of the SEAM framework, calculating the completion rates of your sprints and the achievement rates of your goals is essential. This approach not only provides clarity on your progress but also identifies areas that need improvement, helping you stay aligned with your career vision.

Why **Completion Rates for Sprint Outcomes** Are Important:

- **Shows Collective Performance:** Evaluates the combined effectiveness of all tasks within a sprint, giving a comprehensive view of progress towards the outcome.
- **Identifies Gaps:** Low completion rates indicate areas of concern that may be hindering your overall progress. Reviewing these gaps helps you to improve and to move forward.
- **Helps Make Informed Decisions:** Understanding completion rates empowers you to make informed adjustments to your tasks, ensuring you stay on track.

Why **Goal Achievement Rates** Matter:

- **Big Picture View:** Provides a comprehensive assessment of your progress towards achieving your career vision.
- **Direction and Patterns:** Identifies patterns in your progress to determine if you are on the right path, allowing for course corrections if necessary.
- **Continuous Improvement:** Allows for strategic adjustments and ongoing development by identifying areas needing improvement.

Practical Benefit:

- **Resource Allocation:** Helps determine where to allocate resources more effectively to achieve better results.

Reflection: Embracing Progress and Growth

When reviewing completion rates, like those shown **Figure 4.3.** (e.g., 83% for Sprint Outcome 2.1 and 67% for Sprint Outcome 2.2), you open a window into your journey. Higher rates are a reminder of how far you've come—moments to celebrate. Lower rates, meanwhile, are opportunities to pause, reflect, and consider what might help you move forward. Tracking these rates is not only about progress but about growth, giving you the chance to both celebrate your achievements and find areas to strengthen.

Question: What small steps can you take to make regular check-ins part of your routine? How might this habit support you in staying focused and making adjustments that bring you closer to your goals?

INSIGHT EXERCISE 4.1.
MEASURING MY PROGRESS

Curious to see how your efforts stack up? Keep in mind that each task within a sprint has its own completion date, so not all sprints will finish simultaneously—and the same applies to your overall goals. When you're ready to assess your progress, dive into **Insight Exercise 4.1** to complete Blocks 7 and 8. Continue using My Career Action Plan—the fillable PDF provided in **Insight Exercise 3.1**—to work through these blocks

Access Fillable PDFs for
Insight Exercises at
madeleinewallace.com/resources-ai

MEASURE PART II: ESTABLISHING BENCHMARKS AND INTERPRETING RESULTS

This section guides you in setting robust success criteria and interpreting results when you have completed any of the following blocks:

- **Block 5:** Calculate Percentage of Target Achieved for Each Task
- **Block 7:** Calculate Completion Rate for Each Sprint Outcome
- **Block 8:** Calculate Achievement Rate for Each Goal

To accurately gauge your progress and determine what the numbers from the blocks mean in terms of success, a benchmark or point of reference is essential. These benchmarks often represent best practices or industry standards. In SEAM, we utilize the following benchmarks, which have been proven to help individuals assess their performance effectively.

SEAM'S QUANTITATIVE SELF-PERFORMANCE BENCHMARKS

- **Excellent Performance (80% and above):** This indicates exceeding or meeting the majority of your targets, demonstrating strong achievement.

- **Good Performance (70% to 79%):** Most targets were met, though there might be room for improvement in some areas.

- **Satisfactory Performance (60 to 69%):** While progress is evident, considerable attention needs to be directed towards areas where targets were not met.

- **Needs Improvement (Below 60%):** Falling below 60% suggests significant areas requiring improvement and a potential need to re-evaluate goals or strategies.

Applying Seam's Benchmarks To The Director Of Digital Marketing Example

In **Figure 4.4,** the *Rating* column is introduced to apply SEAM's Self-Performance Benchmarks, assessing each task and sprint outcome for the Digital Marketing Director example. The *% of Target Achieved*, positioned directly to the left of the *Rating* column, serves as the basis for these evaluations.

The columns for *Sprint Outcome, Task,* and *% of Target Achieved* are carried over from **Figures 4.2 and 4.3.** The following discussion highlights key observations derived from the data.

- **Goal 1:** Achieved 62%, which falls within the satisfactory performance range. This indicates that while there has been some progress, certain sprint outcomes still require significant attention to meet the majority of targets.
- **Goal 2:** Achieved 80%, reflecting strong progress and indicating that the goal is on the right track to reach the career vision.

- **Task 2.1.2:** Achieved 80%, demonstrating strong performance that meets the benchmark for excellence.
- **Sprint Outcome 1.3 (Goal 1):** Achieved only 33% of the target, indicating a need for significant improvement. This falls below the 60% threshold, suggesting that a re-evaluation of goals or strategies may be necessary.
- **Sprint Outcome 2.2 (Goal 2):** Achieved 67%, showing progress but also highlighting areas that require further enhancement to meet targets.

Figure 4.4. Summary of Performance for the Digital Marketing Director Example

Goal 1: Become a Director of Digital Marketing at Whole Foods by leveraging proven expertise in social marketing principles and best practices specific to the organic and health-conscious supermarket industry.

Sprint Outcome	Task		% of Target Achieved	Rating
Sprint Outcome 1.1: Gain comprehensive knowledge and practical skills on the latest advancements in generative AI applications in social media marketing.	**Task 1.1.1** Obtain a generative AI Large Language Models (LLMs) certification.		100%	Excellent
	Task 1.1.2 Complete a practical project using generative AI in social media marketing.		100%	Excellent
Completion Rate Sprint Outcome 1.1		Total	100%	Excellent
Sprint Outcome 1.2: Enhance leadership skills and project management techniques for digital marketing.	**Task 1.2.1** Participate in a leadership webinar series tailored for digital marketing managers.		80%	Excellent
Completion Rate Sprint Outcome 1.2		Total	80%	Excellent
Sprint Outcome 1.3: Submit job applications.	**Task 1.3.1** Submit job applications.		33%	Needs Improvement
Completion Rate Sprint Outcome 1.3		Total	33%	Needs Improvement
Goal 1 Achievement Rate		Grand Total	62%	Satisfactory

Figure 4.4. Summary of Performance for the Digital Marketing Director Example (Continued)

Goal 2: Build a portfolio showcasing successful campaigns and marketing solutions that meet both business objectives and the needs of health-conscious customers.

Sprint Outcome	Task	% of Target Achieved	Rating
Sprint Outcome 2.1: Develop, launch, and measure a social media campaign targeting health-conscious customers using generative AI.	**Task 2.1.1** Obtain a generative AI Large Language Models (LLMs)certification.	80%	**Excellent**
	Task 2.1.2 Complete a practical project using generative AI in social media marketing.	80%	**Excellent**
	Task 2.1.3 Launch the campaign, track, and analyze key engagement metrics (likes, shares, comments) to measure effectiveness.	90%	**Excellent**
Completion Rate Sprint Outcome 2.1	**Total**	**83%**	**Excellent**
Sprint Outcome 2.2: Develop case studies highlighting successful marketing campaigns.	**Task 2.2.1** Collect testimonials from previous campaigns.	67%	**Satisfactory**
	Task 2.2.2 Publish the case studies on the company website and social media.	67%	**Satisfactory**
Completion Rate Sprint Outcome 2.2	**Total**	**67%**	**Satisfactory**
Goal 2 Achievement Rate	**Grand Total**	**80%**	**Excellent**

PUTTING RESULTS INTO PERSPECTIVE

Remember, these benchmarks are guidelines. Several factors can influence success rates:

- **Complexity and Difficulty:** Highly challenging or complex goals may warrant a lower completion rate to indicate success. For example, acquiring a new skill like generative AI requires navigating an evolving field with ongoing learning. Reaching 80 % mastery might be exceptional in this context.
- **Contextual Challenges:** Consider unforeseen setbacks beyond your control, discussed in the Envision step (e.g., economic factors, market demand) or personal circumstances (e.g., relocations, family emergencies). Block 6 encourages you to record such challenges and mitigation strategies. These contextual factors should be factored into your evaluation.

This perspective will help you better understand your progress and make informed adjustments to your tasks within each sprint outcome to reach your goals.

YOUR TURN TO INTERPRET YOUR RESULTS

Reflecting on your progress is a critical step in career development. In our hectic and fast-paced lives, it's easy to overlook what we've accomplished or struggle to measure our progress toward our goals. **Insight Exercise 4.2** serves as your wind rose, a compass guiding you towards your career vision by helping you to identify key learnings and to plan for future improvements.

INSIGHT EXERCISE 4.2. MY POST-REFLECTION

- **Review Your Percentages and Apply SEAM's Benchmarks:**
  - Refer to what you completed in **My Career Action Plan** (the Fillable PDF) as part of **Insight Exercise 4.1**, where you worked through Blocks 7 and 8. Examine the completion rates of your tasks, sprint outcomes, and achievement rates for your goals. Using SEAM's benchmarks, rate each percentage in the "Rating" column. For example, if your completion rate is 75%, assign it a rating of "Good Performance."

Interpret and Reflect:

- Complete the **Post-Reflection** section with your insights. Use the guiding questions and **Figure 4.5** to analyze your results after assigning ratings. This reflection helps you understand patterns in your completion and achievement rates, guiding you to make informed decisions and strategic adjustments. By identifying strengths and areas for improvement, you can better navigate challenges, capitalize on opportunities, and align your actions with your career vision.

Figure 4.5. Practical Guidance for Interpreting Results

Consistently Low Percentages Across Goals	• **Identify Root Causes:** Low percentages across multiple goals suggest systemic issues. Review whether your goals are realistic, if you have sufficient resources, and if external factors impact your progress. • **Re-evaluate Strategies:** It may be necessary to adjust your strategies, timelines, or resource allocation. Consider seeking feedback from mentors or peers to gain insights.
Varied Percentages Among Tasks and Sprint Outcomes	• **Analyze Specific Tasks:** If some tasks have higher completion rates than others, identify what is working well and what isn't. Try to apply the strategies that work for the high-performing tasks to the lower-performing ones. • **Address Weak Spots:** Focus on the tasks with lower percentages to understand the obstacles. Are they due to a lack of resources, insufficient skills, or external challenges? Developing targeted solutions for these areas can improve overall performance.
High Percentages Across All Goals and Sprint Outcomes	• **Sustain and Scale:** High percentages across all goals and sprint outcomes indicate strong performance. Identify the strategies and resources responsible for the success and consider how they can be sustained and scaled. • **Innovation and Stretch Goals:** With consistent high performance, you might want to set more challenging stretch goals or explore innovative approaches to push the boundaries of your achievements further.

INSIGHT EXERCISE 4.2: POST-REFLECTION

Sprint Outcome # _____ **Completion Rate:** _____ **%**

_____

_____

Goal # _____ **Achievement Rate:** _____ **%**

_____

_____

- **Question 1:** What were my two key learnings, and how have they contributed to my professional growth?
  - **Purpose:** *Reflecting on what I have learned and how these learnings have enhanced my skills or knowledge is essential for understanding my overall development and planning future steps in my career.*

_____

_____

_____

- **Question 2:** How were my underperforming tasks impacted by external circumstances, family issues, or lack of interest? How can understanding these challenges inform my approach to future challenges, especially in areas where improvement or satisfactory performance was needed?
  - **Purpose:** *This reflection helps me to develop more effective strategies for future challenges by understanding the root causes of obstacles—whether they were external, personal, or due to disinterest. Gaining this clarity enhances my problem-solving skills and strengthens my resilience.*

_____

_____

_____

- **Question 3:** What changes would I make to my next tasks, sprint outcomes, and goals based on what I have learned from this experience?
  - **Purpose:** *Identifying adjustments for future tasks, sprint outcomes, and goals based on past experiences helps ensure continuous improvement and adaptability. Applying lessons learned will make progress towards future sprint outcomes / goals more effective.*

_____

_____

_____

After analyzing your achievements, you will gain clarity on the steps needed to continue progressing toward your career vision.

ADDITIONAL BENCHMARKS OF SUCCESS

Getting things done is important, but how well we do them matters, too. Completion rates, which compare targets with actual results, are like checking off waypoints on a map. While they are important, they don't tell the whole story. Some goals require a deeper dive into quality—how effectively we execute tasks. Your goals can be measured with qualitative benchmarks as well. See the **Qualitative Benchmarks for Career Development** in the Resources section of this chapter.

Another factor of success to note is your satisfaction with your personal life as you implement your career development plan. Career transition can be a stressful time and it is important to maintain a good balance between your professional and personal life. Please see some additional helpful information on doing this in **Strategies for Effective Work-Life Integration** in the Resources section.

SCIENCE SPOTLIGHT
Developing a Digital Mindset

To develop a digital mindset, mastery of all digital skills is not necessary. Instead, Tsedal Neeley and Paul Leonardi (2022) propose a "30 % rule," suggesting that achieving basic fluency in a few key areas is sufficient. By adopting the following three core approaches, individuals and organizations can cultivate the mindset needed to navigate and succeed in the digital era:

Three Core Approaches:

1. **Collaboration:**
   - Effective Collaboration: Work efficiently with both humans and machines.
   - Understanding Technology: Learn how AI and other technologies can enhance human efforts.

2. **Computation:**
   - Digital Fundamentals: Understand the basics of how digital technologies function.
   - Key Areas: Focus on algorithms, data analysis, and coding principles.

3. **Change:**
   - Continuous Learning: Embrace ongoing learning and adaptation.
   - Staying Updated: Keep pace with the constantly evolving digital landscape.

IDEA GEM
Using Distraction to Manage Stress

When I am stressed, I turn to one of the distress tolerance skills from Dialectical Behavior Therapy (DBT) called "distraction" (Linehan, 2014). This technique helps me take my mind off the distressing situation and regain a sense of calm. Here are the ways I incorporate distraction into my life:

- **Activities:** I watch a movie with a good storyline, immersing myself in the plot to forget about my current stressors.
- **Contributing:** I help a friend in my area of expertise, such as running statistics for a project. This intellectual engagement not only distracts me but also gives me a sense of purpose and fulfillment.
- **Comparisons:** Having grown up in a Latin American country with a different standard of living, I often compare my current problems to those I observed back home. This perspective helps me to realize that my issues may be out of proportion and provides context on what is truly important.
- **Emotions:** To elicit laughter and change my emotional state, I set a timer for 15 minutes and watch a funny video. Additionally, I take breaks from social media for two weeks to avoid unnecessary stress.

These distraction techniques are crucial in helping me to manage stress effectively, allowing me to refocus and to handle challenges with a clearer mind.

MEASURE PART III: CULTIVATING A CAREER OF CONTINUOUS GROWTH

Congratulations! Reaching this stage in the SEAM framework for career transformation signifies that you've gained valuable insights about yourself and the future of your industry, or a new industry you're considering. You should now have a solid action plan to establish your place in the current technological evolution. Remember, we live in a constantly changing environment. More importantly, you are now equipped with the insights, skills, and tools from the SEAM framework to successfully navigate any of the Big Three.

You are no longer just a participant in your career but a proactive architect of your future. By embracing continuous career development, you will stay aligned with relevant trends, future directions, and emerging technologies. With SEAM, you can revisit the principles of Snapshot, Envision, Act, and Measure to adapt and thrive in your career and grow professionally. This workbook is a resource for an iterative process that will be as relevant five years from now as it is today.

THE PROCESS FOR CONTINUING THE JOURNEY

1. **Celebrate Successes**
   - **Celebrate Your Wins:** If you have met one or more of your fixed or flexible goals, take time to celebrate and congratulate yourself. Celebrate tangibly with a dinner out with friends, taking an afternoon off for yourself, or buying that special something you've had your eye on.
   - **Revisit and Reflect:** Continue to revisit the SEAM steps as your career progresses and technologies change. Your answers may change, but the method to updating your career vision and working towards your goals will remain the same.
   - **Set New Goals:** If you have met a fixed goal, create another one for the future. Keep moving forward and thrive!
   - **Adapt and Evolve:** If you have met a flexible goal, remember that it will evolve with the Big Three. Use the SEAM steps to revisit the flexible goal and shape it to stay relevant.

2. **Address Unmet Goals**
   - **Iterate and Improve:** If you did not meet your fixed or flexible goal, don't worry. SEAM is an iterative process. By revisiting the work you did, you can make improvements that will lead to your success.
   - **Reexamine and Adjust:** Reflect on the thought process behind drafting your sprint outcomes and how each one contributes to your overall goal. By reviewing your efforts and insights from **Insight Exercise 4.2**, you can easily pinpoint the sprint outcomes that need adjustment.

3. **Perform Snapshot Checks**
   - **Update Your SEAM Career Profile:** Is your career profile still the same? Remember, your SEAM career profile evolves as you learn and grow. It may have already changed! Occasionally, especially when you feel stuck, return to **Insight Exercise 1.6** to update your profile. Viewing your career from a new angle can provide valuable insights and help you to move forward.
   - **Stay Informed:** In the AI era, being a lifelong learner is essential. Schedule a recurring time to review the Big Three: Relevant Trends, Future Directions, and Emerging Technologies. Use **Insight Exercises 1.4 and 1.5** as a starting point to stay motivated and up-to-date. Staying informed ensures you remain adaptable and ahead in the ever-evolving professional landscape.

4. **Envision Again**
   - **Plan New Sprints:** Do you need to plan another exploration sprint? **Visit Figure 2.1** and see if your current career profile recommends a sprint.
   - **Overcome Obstacles:** Have changing internal or external factors hindered your progress? Revisit **Insight Exercises 2.2 and 2.3** to check.
   - **Learn and Adapt:** Review your sprint reflections. Can you learn anything to help you improve progress towards your goal?

5. **Act with Determination**
   - **Refine Outcomes:** Reevaluate your tasks within sprint outcomes to ensure they align with your revised career vision. Make necessary adjustments to stay on course.

- **Optimize Tasks and KPIs:** Thoroughly review your tasks and KPIs. Are they the most effective and efficient means to achieve your goals?
- **Learn from Reflections:** Dive deep into your post-sprint reflections. What valuable lessons can you extract to help you achieve both your flexible and fixed goals more effectively?

6. **Measure Accurately**
   - **Verify KPIs:** Ensure you have selected the most relevant KPIs to accurately measure your progress. Quick Tip: Check if each KPI reflects the critical aspects of your goals and objectives. If a KPI doesn't highlight a key area of importance, consider revising it.
   - **Check Calculations:** Double-check your calculations to confirm that you have correctly determined your percentage of success.
   - **Extract Insights:** Analyze your post-sprint reflections to uncover actionable insights that can drive improvement.
   1. **Review Reflections:** Revisit your post-goal reflections. What lessons can you apply to future goals to enhance your success?

7. **Seek Feedback**
   - **Consult:** At any step of the SEAM framework, seek feedback from a trusted peer, manager, team leader, mentor, or coach. Feedback loops are vital to the SEAM framework because they offer valuable perspectives on your performance and interactions, helping you grow and improve continuously.
   - **Collaborate:** Embrace collaboration as a cornerstone of your professional development. In today's highly connected work environment, teamwork and sharing expertise are essential. Not only do they drive innovation and efficiency, but they also contribute significantly to your personal growth. Engaging with others enhances your skills, broadens your understanding, and prepares you for future challenges.

I encourage you to develop a habit of professional growth throughout your life, not only with SEAM but with everything you encounter. Check out **Developing a Growth Habit** in the Resources at the end of this chapter for my tips on how to do it. Embrace this journey of continuous improvement and keep pushing the boundaries of your potential.

LEARNING LOCK-IN

As you complete the exercises and reflect on the journey you've embarked upon with the SEAM framework, remember that measurement is not the final step but a gateway to continual growth and achievement. Carry forward the momentum you've built here, and always strive to measure your success not just by reaching your targets, but also by the invaluable knowledge and experience you gain along the way.

As you look forward to your career journey, what new opportunities are you most excited to explore, and how will you use the SEAM framework to seize them?

_____

_____

_____

_____

I wish you all the best for a successful career journey, equipped with evolving, future-proof skills that help you realize your career vision now and in the future. Embrace this journey with confidence, curiosity, and a commitment to continuous improvement. We hope you've enjoyed working towards your career transformation with SEAM and we warmly welcome your feedback and shared experiences at: madeleinewallace.com.

Stay inspired, stay determined, and let SEAM guide you towards a fulfilling and impactful career. Remember, the path to success is a continuous journey, and every step you take brings you closer to your ultimate goals.

Chapter 4: Resources

QUALITATIVE BENCHMARKS FOR CAREER DEVELOPMENT

Getting things done is important, but how well we do them matters, too. Completion rates, which compare targets with actual results, are like checking off waypoints on a map. While they are important, they don't tell the whole story. Some goals require a deeper dive into quality—how effectively we execute tasks. This is where qualitative benchmarks come in, measuring the quality of your career journey.

By focusing on both quantitative completion rates and qualitative benchmarks, you gain a richer understanding of your progress and identify areas for continuous development. This allows you to:

- Showcase your true value by demonstrating not just what you completed, but how well you did it.
- Set more meaningful goals that go beyond just checking boxes.
- Impress potential employers or clients with a well-rounded skill set and a commitment to quality.

SEAM'S QUALITATIVE BENCHMARKS

Use a four-point scale and assign categories with 4 = Excellent, 3 = Good, 2 = Satisfactory, 1 = Needs Improvement. Reviewing these alongside completion rates provides a more complete picture of your progress. While using a numerical scale to rate qualitative aspects may seem like a return to numbers, it serves to standardize and clarify the evaluation process. The key difference is that these ratings are based on the quality and depth of your performance, not just task completion.

Example Task a:
Develop Project Management Skills

Quantitative Benchmark for Task a:
Successfully complete two projects on time and within budget (Completion Rate = 2 completed projects / 2 projects = 100%)

Qualitative Benchmark for Task a:
- **Strong Problem-Solving Skills:** Identify and resolve project issues proactively.

Excellent: Effectively solves problems independently.

- **Good:** Solves problems with some assistance.
- **Satisfactory:** Needs considerable assistance to solve problems.
- **Needs Improvement:** Struggles to identify or solve problems.

- **Leadership and Delegation:** Effectively delegate tasks and motivate team members to achieve project goals.
  - **Excellent:** Strong leadership and delegation skills.
  - **Good:** Delegates tasks but may lack motivational skills.
  - **Satisfactory:** Inconsistent delegation and motivation.
  - **Needs Improvement:** Micromanages tasks and struggles to inspire team members.

By assessing both completion rates and qualitative benchmarks, you gain a richer understanding of your project management skills and areas for improvement. This allows you to stand out from the competition and demonstrate your well-rounded capabilities to potential employers or clients.

Remember, career development is a con-tinuous process. By incorporating qualitative benchmarks, you gain valuable insights that help you level up your skills and confidently navigate your career path.

STRATEGIES FOR EFFECTIVE WORK-LIFE INTEGRATION

Friedman (2014) finds that successful in-dividuals often achieve great accomplishments by integrating various aspects of their lives, such as work, home, community, and personal growth, in ways that support and enhance each other. Through trial and error, they discover how their commitments at home and in the community can contribute to their profession-al success. These individuals demonstrate that it is possible to harmonize values, actions, so-cial contributions, and personal development, achieving a balanced and fulfilling life over time rather than daily.

Here are some strategies to help you achieve a more integrated and satisfying work-life balance:

1. **Set Boundaries**
- **Strategy:** Clearly define when work ends and personal time begins. This helps pre-vent burnout and ensures that you have

dedicated time for relaxation and personal activities (Gionta, 2009).

- **Example:** Use a digital calendar to block off personal time, ensuring no work meetings or tasks are scheduled during these periods.
  - **Try This:** Start by blocking off one hour each day for personal time and see how it impacts your well-being.

2. **Prioritize Self-Care**
- **Strategy:** Make self-care a non-negotiable part of your routine. Regular exercise, healthy eating, and mindfulness practices can significantly improve your well-being (Berns-Zare, 2024).
- **Example:** Schedule regular workouts and meal prep sessions to ensure you maintain a healthy lifestyle amidst a busy work schedule.
  - **Try This:** Dedicate 30 minutes each morning to exercise and prepare healthy snacks for the day.

3. **Leverage Technology**
- **Strategy:** Utilize technology to automate repetitive tasks and streamline your workflow. This can free up more time for personal activities and reduce work-related stress (Rogers, 2023).

- **Example:** Use project management tools like Trello or Asana to organize tasks and set reminders, ensuring you stay on top of work without feeling overwhelmed.
  - **Try This:** Set up a project management tool today to plan your week's tasks and see the difference in your productivity.

4. **Maintain Open Communication**
- **Strategy:** Foster open communication with your employer and colleagues about your work-life balance needs. Transparency can lead to more flexible work arrangements and better understanding from your team (Martin, 2021).
- **Example:** Have regular check-ins with your manager to discuss workload and any adjustments needed to maintain a healthy balance.
  - **Try This:** Schedule a meeting with your manager this week to discuss your current workload and any potential adjustments.

STRATEGIES FOR CONTINUOUS PROFESSIONAL GROWTH

Your career isn't a rigid path but a journey of exploration and evolution. Here's how to make growth a habit:

THE ART OF REGULAR REFLECTION

- **Monthly Dinner with Myself:** Every month, I take myself out to a high-end restaurant with a notebook in hand. This solo dinner is a time for self-reflection, where I assess my progress and build my confidence without worrying about others' perceptions. I ask myself questions about my work at Windrose Vision, such as: What's working well? Where can I adjust my approach for better results? For instance, if a specific project is lagging, I identify roadblocks and brainstorm ways to overcome them, such as reallocating resources or adjusting deadlines.
  - **Try It Yourself:** Schedule a monthly dinner date with yourself. Choose a quiet, comfortable place, bring a notebook, and reflect on your progress. Ask yourself questions like, "What's working well?" and "Where can I improve?" Use this time to plan actionable steps for your growth.

SPARKING YOUR CREATIVITY

- **Explore New Horizons:** I live in Washington, DC, and travel frequently, which allows me to regularly engage in activities that stimulate my creativity. Whenever I visit a new city, I make it a point to visit museums. I focus on the paintings and the serene ambiance of the museum, which invites me to see the details of the artwork. With the rise of immersive experiences, it's easier than ever to be transported to another time and place through art. I also enjoy installation exhibitions, which offer unique, interactive experiences that spark my imagination.
  - **Try New Things:** Regularly engage in activities that stimulate creativity. Visit a museum for art inspiration, try new recipes from different countries, start learning a musical instrument, or use an app to learn a new language.

- **Question Everything:** When I'm stuck, I challenge assumptions and look for alternative solutions. I ask myself, "What if...?" and explore the possibilities. I also consider how professionals from different fields might approach the problem by asking, "If I were an engineer, how would I look at this?" or "If I were a physician, what would my perspective be?" Since I can't always know exactly how they would think, I seek solutions in different fields. This interdisciplinary approach is a key part of my training and helps me consider unconventional approaches or technologies that might offer better solutions.

- **Invite You to Reflect:** The next time you're faced with a challenge, ask yourself, "What if...?" and consider how different professionals might tackle the problem. Seek inspiration from other fields to find innovative solutions.

- **Share and Solidify Knowledge:** After attending a conference, I make it a point to share what I learned or the new things I saw with my mentees, spouse, or friends upon my return. I find that this not only helps to solidify the information in my mind but also benefits others by spreading new insights and knowledge.

  - **Encourage You to Share:** After you learn something new or attend an event, share your insights with others. This practice will help reinforce your understanding and spread valuable knowledge to those around you.

REFERENCES

Alghazo, R., Daqqa, I., Abdelsalam, H., Pilotti, M., and Almulhem, H. (2020). *The Impact Of Visualization Techniques On Goal Achievement.* International Journal of Cognitive Research in Science, Engineering and Education. (IJCRSEE).

Berns-Zare, I. (2024, June 3). *5 Steps To Reset Your Work-Life Balance.* Psychology Today. https://www.psychologytoday.com/intl/blog/flourish-and-thrive/202406/5-steps-to-reset-your-work-life-balance

Cialdini, R. B., (2006). *Influence: The Psychology of Persuasion.* Harper Business.

Clear, J. (2018). *Atomic Habits: An Easy & Proven Way to Build Good Habits & Break Bad Ones.* Avery.

Cohn, M. (2005). *Agile Estimating and Planning.* Prentice Hall.

Coutu, D.L. (2002). *How Resilience Works.* Harvard Business Review.

Covey, S. (1989). *The 7 Habits of Highly Effective People: Powerful Lessons in Personal Change.* Free Press.

Deloitte (2022, September 8). *The Skills-Based Organization: A New Operating Model For Work And The Workforce.* Deloitte Insights Magazine. https://www2.deloitte.com/content/dam/insights/articles/us175310_consulting-the-skills-based-org-report/DI_The-skills-based-organization-report.pdf?trk=public_post_comment-text

Deming, E. W. (1986). *Out of the Crisis.* MIT Press.

Denning, S. (2018). *The Age of Agile: How Smart Companies Are Transforming the Way Work Gets Done.* AMACOM.

Ennis, R.H. (1996). *Critical Thinking.* Prentice Hall.

Friedman, S. D. (2014). *What Successful Work and Life Integration Looks Like.* Harvard Business Review.

Gilster, P. (1997). *Digital Literacy.* Wiley Computer Pub.

Gionta, D. (2009, January 30). *Setting Boundaries At Work: Steps To Making Them A Reality.* Psychology Today. https://www.psychologytoday.com/us/blog/occupational-hazards/200901/setting-boundaries-work-steps-making-them-reality

Goleman, D. (1995). *Emotional Intelligence: Why It Can Matter More Than IQ.* Bantam Books.

Goleman, D. (2006). *Social Intelligence: The New Science of Human Relationships.* Bantam Books.

Harkin, B., Webb, T. L., Chang, B. P. I., Prestwich, A., Conner, M., Kellar, I., & Sheeran, P. (2016). *Does Monitoring Goal Progress Promote Goal Attainment? A Meta-Analysis Of The Experimental Evidence.* Psychological Bulletin, 142(2), 198-229.

Kelley, T. and Kelly, D. (2013). *Creative Confidence: Unleashing the Creative Potential Within Us All.* Crown Currency Business.

Lagatree, K. (1998). *Feng Shui at Work: Arranging Your Work Space to Achieve Peak Performance and Maximum Profit* (1st ed.). Villard.

Lenzi, R.N., Korn S.J., Wallace, M., Desmond, N.L., Labosky. P.A. (2020, March 3). *The NIH BEST Programs: Institutional Programs, The Program Evaluation, And Early Data.* FASEB Journal. https://pubmed.ncbi.nlm.nih.gov/31960495/

Leslie, I. (2014). *Curious: The Desire to Know and Why Your Future Depends on It.* Basic Books.

Linehan, MM. (2014). *DBT Skills Training Manual.* Guilford Publications.

Martin, S. (2021, September 16). *How Better Boundaries Can Prevent Burnout.* Psychology Today. https://www.psychologytoday.com/intl/blog/conquering-codependency/202209/how-better-boundaries-can-prevent-burnout

References

Matthews, G. (2007). *The Impact Of Commitment, Accountability, And Written Goals On Goal Achievement.* Psychology Faculty Presentations, (3). https://scholar.dominican.edu/psychology-faculty-conference-presentations/3/

Maxwell, J. C. (2022). *The 21 Irrefutable Laws of Leadership: Follow Them and People Will Follow You.* HarperCollins Leadership.

Microsoft and LinkedIn. (2024, May 8). *AI At Work Is Here. Now Comes The Hard Part.* Work Trend Index Annual Report. https://www.microsoft.com/en-us/worklab/work-trend-index/ai-at-work-is-here-now-comes-the-hard-part

Mark G., Gudith, D., and Klocke, U. (2008, April 6). *The Cost Of Interrupted Work: More Speed And Stress.* Conference on Human Factors in Computing Systems-Proceedings, 107-110. https://dl.acm.org/doi/abs/10.1145/1357054.1357072

Neeley, T. and Leonardi, P. (2022). *The Digital Mindset: What It Really Takes to Thrive in the Age of Data, Algorithms and AI.* Harvard Business Review Press.

Rogers, A. (2023, July 15). *Should You Set Clear Work-Home Boundaries?* Psychology Today. https://www.psychologytoday.com/us/blog/the-wide-wide-world-of-psychology/201705/should-you-set-clear-work-home-boundaries

Schwab, K. (2016). *The Fourth Industrial Revolution. World Economic Forum.* Crown Business.

Stryker, C., and Scapicchio, M. (2024. March 22). *What Is Generative Ai?* IBM. https://www.ibm.com/topics/generative-ai

Wallace, M. (2023). *The SEAM Framework: Achieving Organizational Transformation in 4 Steps.* Fig Factor Media.

World Economic Forum. (2023, April 30). *Future of Jobs Report 2023.* https://www.weforum.org/publications/the-future-of-jobs-report-2023/

ABOUT THE AUTHOR

Dr. Madeleine F. Wallace is an accomplished professional, Amazon Best-selling Author, serial entrepreneur, scientist, investor, and the visionary founder of Windrose Vision. Originally from Peru, she moved to the U.S., where she earned her Ph.D., becoming one of less than 1% of foreign-born Latinas in the U.S. with such a credential. She excels at applying her strategic insights and scientific expertise to solve complex challenges across various domains.

With over two decades of experience, Dr. Wallace has led transformative initiatives in the government, commercial, and nonprofit sectors. As the former Director of the Office of Evaluation and Performance at the National Institutes of Health (NIH), she significantly enhanced the agency's ability to measure and communicate the impact of its research.

Through her firm, Windrose Vision (www.windrosevision.com), Dr. Wallace advises diverse industries on scalability, sustainability, operational excellence, and data optimization. Her SEAM framework (Snapshot, Envision, Act, Measure) is featured in her 2023 Amazon bestseller, *The SEAM Framework: Achieving Organizational Transformation in 4 Steps*, a practical tool designed to facilitate small business digital transformation.

Under Windrose Vision, Dr. Wallace has spearheaded impactful studies for major agencies, including the NIH, National Science Foundation (NSF), Health Resources and Services Administration (HRSA), and the Substance Abuse and Mental Health Services Administration (SAMHSA), focusing on evaluating the effectiveness and impact of their initiatives and programs.

Her extensive research and dedication to mentoring—especially her unwavering support for women entrepreneurs—have driven the adaptation of the SEAM framework for career development, culminating in her 2024 publication, *Thrive in the AI and Digital Age: The SEAM 4 Steps Career Guide and Workbook*. Dr. Wallace is a sought-after speaker and trainer on topics such as strategic planning, organizational change, digital transformation, upskilling, reskilling in the AI era, and evaluating project risk. Her influence extends beyond academia; she actively mentors entrepreneurs and supports the mission of Conectado (www.conect-ado.com). Dr. Wallace's dedication to career transformation is deeply inspired by the resilience of her parents, who successfully navigated their careers through significant technological changes.

Dr. Wallace earned her Ph.D. in Sociology, with a concentration in Demography and Statistics, from the University of Tennessee. She is a distinguished alumna of the Latino Business Action Network (LBAN)'s Business Scaling program at the Stanford University Graduate School of Business, the Goldman Sachs 10,000 Small Businesses Entrepreneurship program at Babson College, and the National Hispana Leadership Institute (NHLI)'s Executive Leadership Program at the John F. Kennedy School of Government, Harvard University.

In her spare time, Dr. Wallace enjoys traveling with her husband, Stephen J. Wallace, also a writer and the author of Hazardous Lies, an Amazon bestseller published in 2023.

APPENDIX

INSIGHT EXERCISE 1.1. MY FUTURE-READY SKILLSET

INSIGHT EXERCISE 1.2. MAPPING MY FUTURE-READY SKILLS WITH THE BIG THREE AND PERSONAL INTERESTS

INSIGHT EXERCISE 1.3. LEARNING FROM REAL-WORLD SCENARIOS

INSIGHT EXERCISE 1.4. ENGAGEMENT IN CAREER DEVELOPMENT ACTIVITIES

INSIGHT EXERCISE 1.5. EDUCATIONAL CAREER GROWTH

INSIGHT EXERCISE 1.6. DEFINING YOUR PROFESSIONAL PROFILE

INSIGHT EXERCISE 2.1. PLANNING AND EXECUTING MY EXPLORATION SPRINTS

INSIGHT EXERCISE 2.2. IMPACT OF POTENTIAL EXTERNAL CHALLENGES

INSIGHT EXERCISE 2.3. IMPACT OF PERSONAL CIRCUMSTANCES

INSIGHT EXERCISE 2.4. CAREER PREPAREDNESS SCENARIO STRATEGIES

INSIGHT EXERCISE 2.5. CAREER VISION

INSIGHT EXERCISE 2.6. GATHERING FEEDBACK

INSIGHT EXERCISE 2.7. IDENTIFYING KEY ELEMENTS IN YOUR CAREER VISION

INSIGHT EXERCISE 3.1. MY CAREER ACTION PLAN

INSIGHT EXERCISE 4.1. MEASURING MY PROGRESS

INSIGHT EXERCISE 4.2. MY POST-REFLECTION

To access Fillable PDFs of the Insight Exercises, scan the QR code or visit https://www.madeleinewallace.com/resources-ai.

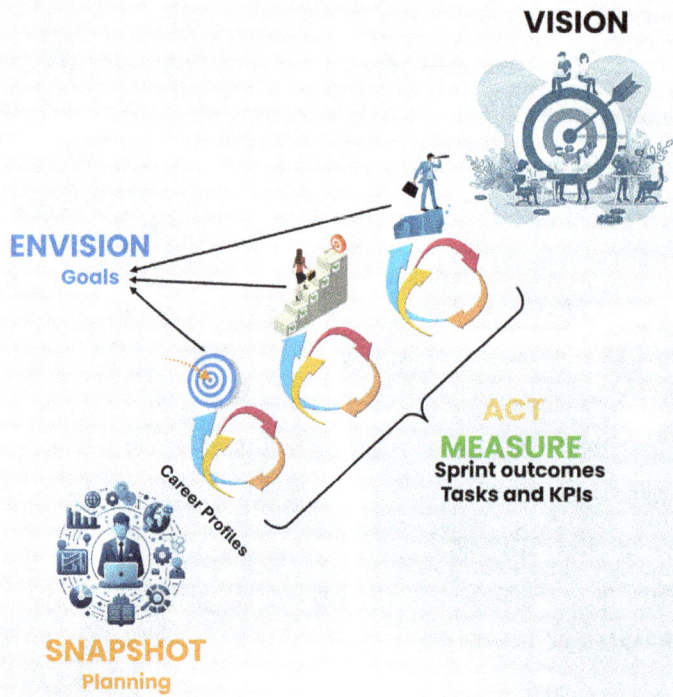

VISION

ENVISION
Goals

Career Profiles

ACT

MEASURE
Sprint outcomes
Tasks and KPIs

SNAPSHOT
Planning

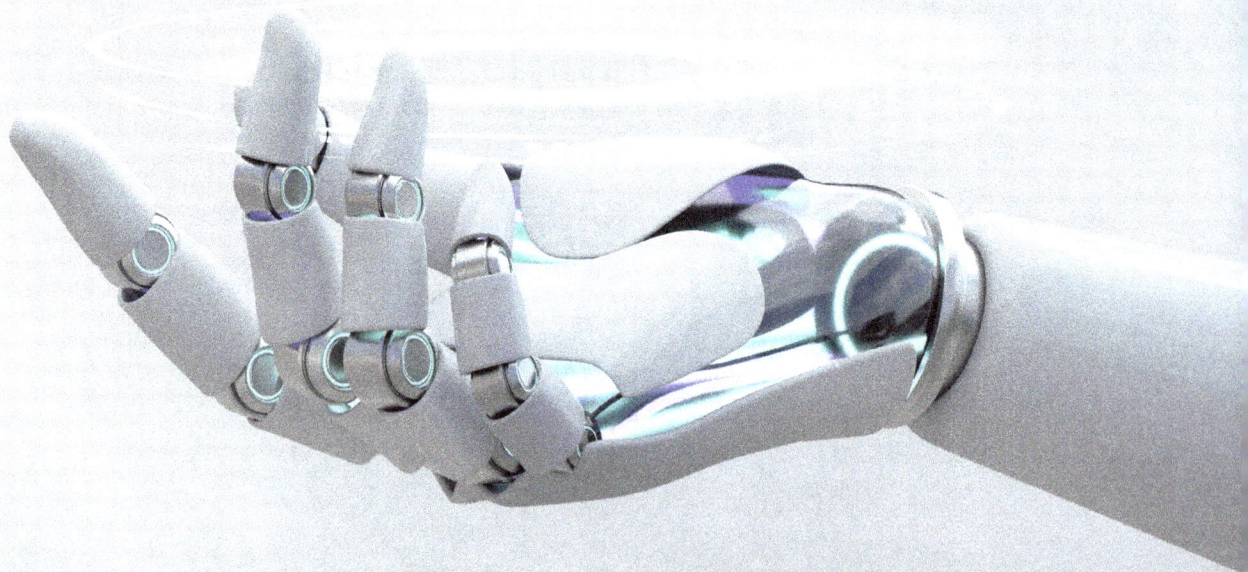

www.ingramcontent.com/pod-product-compliance
Lightning Source LLC
Chambersburg PA
CBHW081456190326
41458CB00015B/5264